MW00325018

eat.delete.

eat.delete.

The 'Anti-quick Fix' Approach

How to get off the weight loss cycle for good

POOJA MAKHIJA

With Gayatri Pahlajani

Collins

An Imprint of HarperCollins Publishers

First published in India in 2012 by Collins
An imprint of HarperCollins *Publishers*

Copyright © Pooja Makhija 2012

P-ISBN: 978-93-5029-234-1
E-ISBN: 978-93-5029-497-0

6 8 10 9 7

Pooja Makhija asserts the moral right
to be identified as the author of this work

All rights reserved. No part of this publication may be reproduced,
stored in a retrieval system, or transmitted, in any form or by any means,
electronic, mechanical, photocopying, recording or otherwise,
without the prior permission of the publishers.

HarperCollins *Publishers*
A-75, Sector 57, Noida 201301, India
1 London Bridge Street, London, SE1 9GF, United Kingdom
Hazelton Lanes, 55 Avenue Road, Suite 2900, Toronto, Ontario M5R 3L2
and 1995 Markham Road, Scarborough, Ontario M1B 5M8, Canada
25 Ryde Road, Pymble, Sydney, NSW 2073, Australia
195 Broadway, New York, NY 10007, USA

Tests in 'The Questions Nobody Asks' designed by Mindtemple
Book Design by Inkspot Inc.
Nourish Logo by khatri.deepa@gmail.com

Typeset in 11/14 Arno Pro
Jojy Philip New Delhi 110015

Printed and bound at
Thomson Press (India) Ltd

Contents

This book is dedicated to all those who have regained their excess weight as fast as they lost it. Who somehow think weight loss is tied to a wedding, a reunion, a hot date or a calendar. Who think stringent timelines are 'motivating'. Who make food the enemy. Who are so worried and anxious about the results, they forget how special, unique and wonderful they are.

To them I say: What's Your Rush?

Runners pounded the road in the cool light of a January morning. The end was almost in sight. A sea of people cheered the motley crew of athletes who had come together to run the annual Mumbai Marathon. Doctors, lawyers, CEOs, a former beauty queen, housewives and students had all come to take part in what would become one of the biggest physical tests of their lives.

For many, this was the end of a journey that had started months – or years – before the day of the race. Some had come from small towns with limited facilities for training. Some had battled illnesses. Whatever motivated them – whether it was the joy of pushing their body to the limit or the satisfaction of achieving a lifelong goal – they all had one thing in common. They weren't looking back to see who was behind them. They weren't looking ahead to see who was ahead of them. They simply looked up. But not at the clock with its red, ticking numbers. As they crossed the finish line – that threshold between failure and success – they focused on six big letters.

F-I-N-I-S-H

They did it. They had finished.

That was their victory.

As children, we were taught that races are there to be won. It's all about coming first because there is no place for second place. We were never taught that finishing, or just sticking to the plan, is a reward in itself.

Long-lasting weight loss is not a sprint; it's not something that needs to be won. Like a marathon, it is simply a journey of endurance. The only difference is that it is a journey to a destination of *your* choice at a pace set by *your* body. Your job is just to reach the finish line.

I wrote this book because I am deeply concerned about the way people pit time against their bodies. We are in such a rush to look good for our wedding, a reunion, a conference or an event that we crash-diet and stress ourselves out, only to eventually put the weight back on again. We push our bodies to their limit because time is suddenly more important than our digestive systems, hearts, brains, circulation, breathing and energy levels. But when time wins, our bodies often lose.

but when time wins, our bodies often lose

Why do we make weight loss a race against time? Where are we going that we're in such a rush? Or is it a question of trust? Do we put such high expectations on our bodies because we're control freaks? Do we control our bodies from the outside because we do not trust our bodies to do the right thing on the inside?

This book is 'The Anti-quick Fix Approach' because years of solid research and, more importantly, your body, will tell you that there is no such thing as a shortcut to stable weight loss. If you want to increase your metabolism, if you want health and wellness, if you want your energy back, if you want to keep the weight off for good or if you simply want your body to respond with thanks and appreciation, there are few choice routes from the starting gun to the finish line and everyone has to take the same path. However, I'm not saying it will take you forever to lose the weight. While this is the Anti-*quick* Fix, I will still provide you with ways to 'fix' your weight problem within a medically recommended timeframe.

What I don't want is for you to make weight loss this complicated, long-winded journey where food – and common sense – becomes your enemy. In this book, I will show you how to provide your body with enough fuel to cross the finish line, and share tips and strategies that will allow you to lose and keep the weight off. What I do want is for you to have fun and enjoy the process. You will be surprised at how much you can eat. You will be surprised at how much you *have* to eat.

But right now, at the start of your own personal journey, as you turn the pages of this book, I want you to slow down and start to appreciate yourself. Don't curse the thighs you got from your mother, or blame your father for your 'tendency' to put on weight. Don't examine every pore that's 'too big' or breasts that are 'too small'. You're uniquely you. And you're uniquely beautiful.

We have enough expectations to live up to. From husbands or wives, from our friends, from our work, from our children, from our parents, from our in-laws, from life. Take the stress out of weight loss and breathe, get on with your life, love yourself. Your body is your friend. It will get you your weight loss. It will do what's best for you. And the sooner you realize that, the happier – and lighter – you will be.

The Quick Fix

You have six weeks to lose those 8 kilos. And your Time. Starts. Now.

We're not the only ones putting pressure on ourselves. This is how weight loss is being marketed. Everything is sold in time-bound 'packages'. There are monthly packages, weekly packages, yearly packages in which you can lose 5 kilos in a month or 10 kilos in two. The Quick Fix seems to be the ultimate solution for people who want to lose weight NOW, with the implied promise that if they follow the programme to the T, their lives will change forever.

Rapid weight loss...

...looks like this:

'Lose 6 kilos in three weeks!'

'The seven-day diet'

'From fat to fit: eight weeks to get that bikini bod'

'The five-day detox'

...sounds like this:

'Make her lose 10 kilos fast. The boy is coming down from New York in two months.'

'Pooja, it's a ten-year reunion and I've had two kids since college. Help!'

'I can't go to Goa looking like this. It's my best friend's wedding!'

...and could make you feel like this:

Irritable, weak, hungry, depressed, fatigued, faint, constipated, deprived, dehydrated

And all of it is usually for nothing. In the case of rapid weight loss, what goes down will come up. When you crash-diet, or even when you have unrealistic expectations of what your body can do, you could ultimately end up with these:

Reduced sex drive, sinus problems, hair loss, muscle atrophy, seizures, acne, gallbladder disease, Anorexia nervosa, bulimia, malnutrition possibly leading to death

In other words, if weight is the only thing you gain back, you can consider yourself lucky.

I don't mean to sound all gloomy, but as a nutritionist I cannot emphasize enough the perils of the Quick Fix. Even the most sensible of us have fallen prey to a shortcut or two. And it's not just about the food. There are diet pills, liposuction, creams, massages, drinks, fat burners, EMS (Electrical Muscle Stimulation) machines, appetite suppressants, the list is endless. But where there seems to be a quick, magical solution to those stubborn thighs or flabby abs, there are also inherent side effects that you are not always informed about. Sometimes hiding behind the Big Loss is the Small Print.

Some may argue that tight timelines are a big motivator, others say that a goal is the only tangible way to achieve weight loss. But what essentially happens with tough deadlines is that they are almost always accompanied by a sense of failure because we tend to focus on what we *haven't* lost. So when we lose 5 kilos in two months, and not in one, we are disappointed because we have not lost more when, in fact, we should be delighted that we have lost 5. That's 5 kilos less that you carry around. That's 5 kilos less pressure on your heart. You're breathing easier, walking faster, feeling better. Celebrate that. Weight loss is not the only way to measure the success of a lifestyle change.

I'm not saying you don't need to work towards something. But we need to understand the difference between deadlines and targets. Or time versus goals. If you have a wedding and you have 10 kilos to lose, give yourself some wiggle room. Be organized and realistic. It is not medically recommended to lose more than half-kilo to a kilo a week, and my meal plans for my clients are designed accordingly. Don't make it impossible for yourself, and always be happy with what you've achieved. And your goal weight? If you eat smart and stay active, you will eventually reach it. What's your rush?

The Anti-quick Fix

So why do we gain weight? Why are we unable to shake it off? If it were as simple as knowing what to eat and what not to eat, wouldn't we all be skinny by now? It doesn't matter who you are or where you come from, losing weight seems to be a universal struggle for most of us. A struggle marked by roller-coaster rides on the weight loss train, in which we lose, gain, lose, gain, with the hope that somewhere down the line, we'll strike gold.

But it doesn't have to be this complicated. And it doesn't have to be a struggle. Kilos don't accumulate overnight. We gain weight because of definite reasons and it's not just about what we eat. Perhaps addressing these issues is the key to keeping the weight off.

It would be very easy for me to start this book off with words like 'metab', 'calorie', 'boiled', 'baked' or 'steamed'. It's what I am trained to do: give nutritional advice. But in my years of practice, I have found that this is not the best way to start your journey to weight loss. I will not immediately jump into what or how you should eat. I will not plunge into calorie charts, BMR calculators, or advice on how to cook. No, that's not how we start this book.

In fact, food is not the starting point at all.

Have you ever thought about WHY you are gaining weight? Food is a very important component of weight gain, but to say that you are overweight because you eat incorrectly is like saying that you are unwell because you have a fever. You aren't wrong. But in so many cases, isn't the fever just a symptom of a larger problem?

Think about it: what if weight gain is just a symptom? A symptom not only of how we eat food, but how we treat food? A symptom not only of how we cook food, but how we look at food? What if losing weight doesn't begin with what's on your plate but with what's on your mind? Maybe understanding why we eat is the best place to start to understand why our numerous attempts to 'diet' have failed. And maybe, just maybe, we struggle with losing weight time and time again because by *only* going on a diet, by *only* checking what we eat, by *only* anxiously restricting our intake, we address *only one* part of a bigger problem.

> What if losing weight doesn't begin with what's on your plate but with what's on your mind?

The Anti-quick Fix is a mind-body approach to weight loss, conceived to tackle weight gain from the ground up so you can deal with the root of the problem. This is probably the first time in India that a weight loss book written by a nutritionist has inputs from mental health experts in an attempt to pinpoint key reasons for weight gain. I have collaborated with one of India's most respected psychiatrists, Dr Anjali Chhabria, and her team at Mindtemple, and with Tara Mahadevan, a qualified nutrition and health psychologist, in an effort to help you re-think your attitudes to food and weight loss.

To Anti-quick Fix Your Weight Loss Is to

Know	Trust
Invest	Finish

I've divided this book into four parts:

Know

First, the diagnosis. What's holding up your weight loss? To make long-lasting changes, to ensure that the weight stays off, we need to understand the underlying causes behind why we gain weight in the first place. We begin by trying to understand our relationship with food – our habits, the way we look at food and the importance we give it in our lives. Then I'm going to make you pick up a pen and take a few tests (nothing dull and boring, I promise!) to see if you are prone to eating when you're angry or sad or bored and also to see if you are truly *ready* to lose weight. Finally, I will give you the tools to change your relationship with food – and show you how to mentally gear yourself to adopt healthy food habits – so that you never have to 'diet' another day in your life.

Trust

What does the body do with the food you eat? How do you burn calories? Trust gives you the inside story of the inner workings of your body so that you realize it is a complex, beautiful machine, which is always working for YOU. Trust hopes to restore your faith in your own body so you can be assured that if you're eating and doing the right things, there is no way you won't reach your goals.

Invest

Invest will give you nutritional toolkits to help you lose weight. This includes counselling on nutritional intake, meal plans and tons of info on how to eat efficiently.

Finish

Get started and then flounder? All set on Day 1 but completely deflated by Day 10? In Finish, we will get you up to speed with some common speed bumps along the way. I have worked with a nutrition and health psychologist and with my clients to help you design strategies for staying on track. I will also give you nutritional advice on how to maintain your new body so that you can always be in the best shape of your life. Victory is closer than you think.

When it comes to weight loss, I want you to take the same pride a marathoner takes in crossing the finish line. If you are here to 'beat', 'win', 'compete', 'compare', you are measuring yourself against people, bodies, deadlines that are not yours. I don't want you to look over your shoulder. Forget about who's catching up with you. Forget about who's running ahead. Your job is to finish. Be a 'finisher'. That will be your victory.

Pooja Makhija
Mumbai
2012

KNOW

Food and Me

I, Ghee, Myself

You can't escape it. It's wherever you go. It's in the new malls with their international food chains. It's in the home-delivery flyers delivered to your doorstep that make you want to reach for the phone and order NOW. It's on TV, it's advertised at the back of your movie ticket, it's in your face when **food** is you're walking to the station or hailing a cab. Let's everywhere face it. Food is everywhere.

And if it's not in our face, it's on our mind. Have you noticed how much of our lives revolve around food? We channel a lot of energy towards it. We talk about what to eat for dinner while we're eating lunch. We plan road trips and get out of the city just to have 'the-best-kebabs-in-the-world' from that one roadside dhaba. We watch food reality shows, cookery shows, buy exotic ingredients and spend money on experiencing the best that world cuisines have to offer. Don't get me wrong – it's loads of fun learning about different world cuisines, but it really doesn't help keep our weight down.

According to the World Health Organization (WHO), about 1.5 billion adults (20 and older) in the world were overweight in 2008[1] with over 200 million men and nearly 300 million women diagnosed as obese – a phenomenon that was probably unheard of just a hundred years ago when the problem, ironically, was that there was not enough food. Clearly, it has never been harder

---

[1] 'Obesity and Overweight, Fact sheet No. 311', http://www.who.int/mediacentre/factsheets/fs311/en/accessed on 10/1/12

to lose weight. Then again, it has never been easier. For every dish that's drowning in oil, there is a healthier, leaner version. There are special foods for people with diabetes, for those who are lactose intolerant, for vegans, and there are organic foods with no MSG, additives or preservatives. There are also gyms, slimming centres, nutritionists, exercise classes, jogging tracks and countless products, solutions and companies that gain from your weight gain.

Why is it that so many of us struggle with weight loss? Why is it that we fail time and again? Could the problem lie in the way we treat food – do we go beyond treating it as a way to nourish or fuel ourselves? Could it be that our relationship with food substitutes other relationships in our lives? Could it be that we give food far more importance than it deserves?

If our relationship with food is complicated, our relationship with weight loss will be complicated too. How can we lose weight if we treat food like a crutch, to be used and abused in times of emotional distress (and isn't emotional distress a certainty)? How can we shed those extra kilos if food largely dictates where we go, how we behave and who we spend time with?

Let's explore some common relationships most of us may have with food. The reason I talk about this first is because I believe that unless these relationships are managed effectively, any chance of being slimmer remains slim. While there is a good chance that, on some level, everything in this chapter will apply to you, the important thing to note is just how strong these relationships are so that you are better equipped to lose the weight you want to. And you *will* lose weight when you stop treating food as the ultimate destination when what you should be doing is treating it as fuel for the journey.

Food As Entertainment

Food is the new social currency. We don't meet our friends for walks, shows and movies as often as we meet them for brunches, dinners, lunches and buffets. We live in a time when making plans has become more about making reservations. We learn our dishes, get to know our ingredients and experiment with world and nouvelle cuisine, because that's become a sign of who we are. From being a sidebar to entertainment, food has become entertainment. And with fine dining, food has become a finely crafted passion, with fussy celebrity chefs leading the charge.

Food is also one of the most complicated relationships that exist. Historically and culturally, food and social interaction are connected. We have always used food as a way to celebrate, remember, comfort, love and mourn together and we have been conditioned to do this over thousands of years. Our fondest memories would probably be associated with our grandma's dahi wadas or the first cake mummy baked for us. It's not an easy relationship to either understand or separate ourselves from.

So I'm not asking you *not* to meet your friends and family over meals. But it could be very difficult to lose weight if you don't make changes to the way you interact socially. If you give food the same entertainment value as a movie or show, or if food is how you pass your time, your body *will* hit back with heart disease, gastro-intestinal infections, acidity, bloating, pre-diabetes and obesity. If not worse.

It is a proven fact that we eat more in the presence of others. Social pressures make us drink recklessly and consume more than we should. Why do women gain weight after they get married? Studies suggest that newly married women eat with husbands who have larger appetites and they are subconsciously trying to match up to them.

Reduce the importance of food in your social life. Take it down a notch. Skip lunch at a fancy, high-priced restaurant. Catch up with your friends over coffee instead. You'll eat less. Call those distant relatives home for chai instead of dinner. If you have kids, meet other friends with their kids and go to the park together. Want to double date with another couple? Forget meeting over drinks or dinner. Instead, go bowling or catch a movie.

You see what you're doing here? You're meeting the same people, spending the same amount of time with them, and losing weight in the process. A dinner takes, what, 90 minutes? So will tea or coffee. Calorie intake over dinner? At least 1200. Calorie intake over coffee or tea? If you don't order a high-cal beverage with whipped cream, you won't be consuming more than 100 to150 calories. See the difference? And I'm not even going into how much money you will save.

Food-free Activities

Walks

Movies, plays, concerts (without unhealthy foods and

sugary drinks)

Play dates at the park or beach

Tea

Coffee

Spa dates (manicures, pedicures, massages)

Shopping

Bowling

Video games

Amusement parks

Museums, art galleries, special events

Re-organize Your Diary

How often do I use food as entertainment?
_____ / week
How many times can I socialize using non-food
or low-food activities?
_____ / week

Food As Escape

We've all been there. We have searched endlessly for solutions to life's problems at the bottom of a bag of potato chips. We've looked for God at the end of a stack of pakodas. We've tried to find the true meaning of life in decadent, rich chocolate. But when it's done frequently and excessively, without us realizing it, emotional eating can affect weight, health and overall well-being. Using food as a way to *always* escape our feelings is a tried-and-tested way of making sure we'll never get back into shape. It's also one of the hardest habits to break.

A common myth about emotional eating is that it's initiated by negative feelings. While people do turn to food when they're stressed out, lonely, sad, anxious or bored, they also do so in love, excitement and happiness. Remember how your grandfather used to give you chocolate as a reward for being a good child? Or when your mum made your favourites when you did well in your exams? Studies[2] have shown that emotional eating is behaviour that we

_____

[2] 'Forget "Emotional Eating"…Think "Learned Eating"', http://www.wlslifestyles.com/all-blogs/warren-l-huberman-phd/20090523540/forget-emotional-eatingthink-learned-eating.php, accessed on 21/2/12

have learned, through which we develop the habit of reaching out for the same foods in happy or sad moments.

It also doesn't help that certain foods are designed to be harder to resist. For example, chocolate has a common mood elevator which produces a high similar to the one you feel when you're in love or on top of the world. Certain foods are embedded with natural or man-made chemicals that make you happy. Your brain starts to associate that food with 'happiness' or 'celebration' and you reach for it the next time you want that feeling.

Emotional eating is pointless because the same high you get with chocolate or another favourite food will be reversed an hour or two later when your sugar levels crash. Which is why, in so many cases, binges make you feel worse than when you started. You also start to feel guilty about binge eating, and sometimes use food again as a way to deal with that guilt. It's a vicious cycle. And it doesn't address what's really bothering you.

It has been said that nothing in life is permanent except change. Well, in today's times, you could say that nothing in life is permanent except stress. It's always going to be there. And eating our stress away with chocolates and samosas isn't going to help.

Now for some good news. If emotional eating is thought to be *learned* behaviour, you can also modify it. It's just about replacing food with something else as a way to deal with your problems. Case in point: a friend with a weight problem, Sahil, took to running for an hour daily to get over a traumatic break-up because he had two options – he could drink and go mad thinking about her or he could find another way to burn the extra emotional energy. He lost 30 kilos.

Upset? Knit. Excited? Go dancing. Depressed? Call a friend and talk. The difference between keeping it off and gaining it all back can sometimes boil down to how you cope with life's ups and downs. Unlearning emotional eating may not be an easy process but it is possible and it starts with being aware of what's going on. You have to learn to differentiate between physical hunger and emotional hunger and identify the triggers that push you to eat when you aren't hungry.

In the next chapter, I will make you test yourself to see whether you are an emotional eater, and what to do when you are about to reach for comfort food. If food is indeed your escape, healing this particular relationship with food is one of the most effective ways to look the best you ever have.

Food As Your Boss

This is the most toxic relationship with food we could possibly have. The problem with having food as your boss – or food addiction – is that the relationship isn't even about food any more. It's about control and about who or what has it. We wake up and eat food, think food, cook food, talk food and dream food. We devote time, energy, resources and emotions to it. We binge endlessly and often eat beyond the point of being comfortably full. Food is nice to look forward to. But we should never be caught in a situation where it determines how we act and how we look. And we don't want to be faced with the reality of knowing that every diet we get on will be powerless in front of it.

Laila was a client whose life was dominated by food. She weighed 103 kilos, and her cravings governed her life. She literally went where the food took her. She was obsessed with thoughts of eating, cooking or buying food. Once, she drove a distance of 200 km because she wanted a certain kind of batata vada. She was pre-diabetic, couldn't walk up more than a flight of stairs at a time, and hated shopping because nothing fit. But weight gain was not the only problem here. If food calls all the shots, is that the life you really want to have?

Food addiction is maladaptive and, like any other addiction, it is harmful to a person's well-being. If it's left untreated, food can be the boss not just of your life but of your health, and can lead to **fire your boss** diabetes, high cholesterol, heart disease, sleep apnea, depression, hypertension, kidney disease and stroke. While this is not meant to alarm those who are helpless in the face of food, it is essential to address this problem if you feel it forms a pattern you just cannot escape. In the next chapter, we're going to gauge whether you are being controlled by your cravings and tell you how to fire your boss.

Food As Seduction

Here you are, on your way to work or window-shopping and BAM! Five minutes later you suddenly find yourself face-deep in rich, creamy ice-cream. Or a gooey chocolate brownie. Or a piping hot samosa filled with spicy potato goodness. You don't even know how it happened. Was it the glorious smell of fresh waffle cones that made you do a U-turn? Was it the six-foot poster of the brownie that looked so happy drowning in molten chocolate? Or were you simply doing a good deed: that samosa looked lonely sitting there by itself. Maybe seemingly innocent factors played a big role in your decision to eat. Or maybe you were seduced.

The reason why so many of us struggle with weight loss is that the environment around us doesn't always support it. For everyone who is watching his or her weight, there seems to be someone who isn't. It sometimes feels like we are alone in our weight loss efforts, in a world where colleagues order in cheesy pizzas on the second day of our new diet or we're invited to a wedding where the chicken or paneer is stewing in a mouth-watering gravy swimming in oil.

Advertising just makes it worse. How delicious those burgers look on TV with cheese and mayo oozing out of them! Your mouth starts watering, your hunger pangs go into overdrive and the helpful phone number on the screen can make you dial your way into unhealthy decisions. The manner in which products are sold to you are both an art and a science – there are people who have dedicated their lives to understanding buying behaviour – and many brands will do anything just so you can buy, buy, buy!

Packaging is made bright and loud so you are more likely to pick it up. Chocolates are placed next to cash registers so you can make impulsive buying decisions. Junk food is put on the lower shelves so kids can put them in the shopping cart without the parents realizing it. And some brands market directly to children, who pester their parents till they give in, leaving more junk food lying about the house.

IS FAT CONTAGIOUS?

Is there a chubby 'virus'? Research increasingly suggests that who you know or who you're friends with has an impact on your own weight. In 2007, Harvard Medical School researchers discovered that a person's risk of being obese rose to 57 per cent if they had a friend of the same sex who was also obese. And between mutual close friends, the chance of becoming obese rose three times to 171 per cent.

Researchers theorize that as people around us get fatter, we change our perception of what it means to be at a particular weight. So if people around us are gaining weight, it influences our standards of what is acceptable. While it doesn't mean that we need to dump friends who are at a higher weight, it does mean that we also need to keep people around us who are healthy and watching what they eat, so that we can keep our inspiration close to us.[3]

---

[3] http://now.tufts.edu/articles/being-fat-contagious, accessed on 23/4/12

Even if you close your eyes and ignore the signs, there are people who bring it to your attention. Observe what happens the next time you place an order at a restaurant or coffee shop. If you ask for a simple cup of coffee, you will be asked if you want 'flavours' or if you want to upsize it for just '20 rupees more'. If you're ordering take-out, the nice lady on the phone asks you if you want it 'with single cheese or double cheese' (you then forget that you also have the option of '*no* cheese'). It may add to the taste and be more 'value for money' but if you upsize or add more fattening ingredients, the calories automatically get upsized too.

In the production of wholewheat pasta or muffins, some manufacturers use a relatively small amount of wheat flour but in just enough quantities to allow them to list 'wholewheat' as one of the ingredients. So you may think you're eating a healthy muffin, but you're not. And this goes for a whole range of products categorized as 'health food'.

Always remember that you are being seduced.

So what do you do with this information? Well, if you're trying to lose weight in this environment (as most of us are), you need to be aware of the kinds of barriers you might encounter on your weight loss journey. I just want you to be conscious of the fact that the dieting environment *can* be hard, even though the tools to lose weight aren't.

But things aren't all gloomy: almost every dish soaked in oil has a low-fat twin. There are more healthy meals than ever before. There are more options for exercise. We live in a far more health-conscious environment than we ever did. So, while losing weight may never have been this hard, it has also never been this easy.

Food As Waste

We are Indians. We hate waste. We reuse, hand down and recycle clothes, toys and even milk packets till they've been squeezed to the last drop. The three magic words in our vocabulary are not 'I Love You' but 'Value for Money'. It's just who we are.

And right on top of the list of things-not-to-waste is food. We are culturally ingrained to finish what we have been served. Children are rewarded if they 'clean' their plates and we have been socially conditioned to believe that we are good guests if we eat properly at weddings and events.

But eating because you don't want it to go to waste is one of the sneakiest ways in which the kilos pile on. When we serve ourselves, especially at buffets or dinner parties, we make decisions with our eyes. We spend the rest of the meal forcefully pushing food down our throats, whether we need it or not.

Picture it: you're at the end of a yummy dinner at a restaurant and you've got three spoonfuls of rice, a couple of pieces of fried potato and a bit of butter chicken left over. Because you don't want this to go to waste, you forcefully overload your system with 200 extra calories. Even if you do this just once a week – and if you don't work off the extra bit – you have already gained over a kilo in the year without realizing it! See what I mean? Sneaky.

And it's not just what you put on your own plate. Women finish off their family's leftovers and ingest hundreds of calories every day, just so they have the satisfaction of knowing that all the khana was over. Let's assume for argument's sake that a woman polishes off 100 extra calories she doesn't need every day. That's 36,500 extra calories eaten in the year. It takes 3500 calories to gain a pound of weight. The noble desire of not wanting food to go to waste has made this woman gain almost 5 kilos in the year. *Five kilos!*

Make the distinction between what you want and what you need. If food is in your body when it doesn't need to be, it's getting wasted already. Find creative uses for leftovers. Reuse them, donate them. Your dinner is done. Be okay with the idea of waste. To ensure that you don't eat food that your body doesn't need:

👍 DO go easy on serving yourself. You can always re-assess your need when you've eaten what's on your plate.

👎 DON'T finish off anyone else's meal. If they've left it, it's for them to finish.

👍 DO re-use leftovers as creatively as possible.

👎 DON'T worry if food sometimes goes to waste. It's really not the end of the world.

👍 DO cook keeping quantities in mind. Not only will you save calories but also groceries, gas and money.

👎 DON'T forget to order smart when you're eating out. Ask the waiter about portion sizes. You can always order more in the middle of your meal.

Food As Enemy

When we hear the word 'diet', the association with deprivation is so strong that we immediately assume it's going to be about deletion and not addition. Many of us, when we want to lose weight, make food the enemy by starving or depriving ourselves to the point where we are punishing our bodies. Or we single out one food group like carbs or fat, making that the enemy and ignoring it completely. Or we make impractical lifestyle changes like drinking the juice of bitter gourd mixed with pumpkin seeds soaked in flaxseed oil. Can you drink that the first thing in the morning? I can't.

Then there are those for whom all foods are the enemy. Eating disorders are on the rise and many people spend their entire lives in the relentless pursuit of thinness, often at the cost of both their physical and emotional health. Disorders like Anorexia nervosa and bulimia hit those who have low self-esteem, are insecure about their ability to find a partner, are heavily influenced by the media, have been exposed to trauma, have been overweight in the past, or even those who work in the demanding industry of beauty.

All food was not born equal. We get that. When you're trying to lose weight there will definitely be certain foods and preparations that you have to avoid. But the same food can be re-integrated into your meals once you reach your goal. And just as you can't make food your boss, you should never make food your enemy. It isn't. It is an ally, a partner, a friend. By punishing yourself with fad diets, fad foods or restricting yourself to one or two food groups, you not only harm yourself, you also make the same foods turn on your body.

Food can be moody. It can alter nutrition and fat content just by the way it's prepared. You can lose weight with rice if you steam it, boil it or bake it. It's obviously not going to help you lose weight if you soak it in ghee or make it sweet. Potatoes are a superb and complete source of complex carbohydrates but you can completely rule out *food* can *be* moody any benefits if you've deep-fried them. Tomato juice is best when freshly made and consumed. But you can forget about nutritive value if it comes out of a pack.

What if I tell you that losing weight is not about deletion, it's about addition? What if I tell you that losing weight is not about upheaval, it's about adjustment? And what if I tell you that losing weight is definitely not about dieting, it's about making permanent changes to your eating habits? If it feels too hard, too strict, too complex and alienates you from your friends, family and yourself, you are doing it wrong. So don't let food be your enemy…

Food Should Be Your Friend

This is the end goal. The prize. THIS is what I want you to work towards. The fabulous, mature, mutually respectful relationship which you can have with the food in your life. You need to strive towards that happy medium where you don't abuse your body with food and food in turn doesn't abuse your body. It's about balance, proportion, percentage and perception. It's about care, tolerance, respect and patience.

Food is what gives you life. It fuels you, cures you and heals you. It should never be regarded with fear or be treated as a lover, boss or enemy. It should be a friend you call on whenever *you* need to, and an ally to nourish and fuel a healthy lifestyle. Long-term weight loss is really about working *with* food and not against it, using the best it has to offer and discarding what doesn't work for you. Long-term weight loss is also about finding taste and flavour in everything you eat. Because the journey from fat to fit should be enjoyed, cherished and loved. And that is the least you deserve.

The Questions
Nobody Asks

Boil. Bake. Steam. Grill. Calorie. Carbs. Diet. If only weight loss was just about the food.

Let's say you want to lose 10 kilos. What do you do? You make calls, get recommendations and go to the slimming centre/ gym/ doctor/ nutritionist/ fitness studio or find a weight loss solution of your choice. The first thing any reputed gym or nutritionist will ask you to do is to fill out a lengthy questionnaire. The questions look a bit like this:

- ❏ Do you have a history of hypertension/ blood pressure or diabetes?
- ❏ Have you ever been asked to stop an exercise programme by your doctor?
- ❏ Are you pregnant?
- ❏ Have you ever felt dizzy or breathless while exercising?
- ❏ What are the medications you are currently taking?

As you tick the boxes, you already start to feel better – and rightly so – because you have now begun your weight loss journey. Yes, these are questions *everybody* asks. And they should.

A month or two later, you've all but given up on your quest to reach your goal weight. You didn't follow the diet properly, or you could only go to the gym twice a week. You start to blame yourself for not having the willpower or not being truly committed to the cause. Your thinner wife/ husband/ son/ daughter/ mother/ father/ friend has told you that you are 'wasting money on expensive gyms' and that 'you just need to go for walks, like I do'. And you're right back where you started. With a lighter… wallet.

Sounds familiar? Why is the result almost always the same? I believe that while it is crucial to ask questions about your physical state of being, these questions don't help you assess your mental state of being. What about the questions nobody asks? About what you actually feel about food? About your expectations, about how – or like who – you want to look? Did you know that unrealistic expectations about the end result can kill a weight loss plan like nothing else can? Or that 'stress eating' can disrupt your best intentions to eat healthy? Or that no matter how hard you try, if you are chronically addicted to food, no gym or nutritionist will be able to help you?

Insanity has been defined as doing the same thing over and over again and expecting different results. Before you throw up your hands and completely abandon the idea of losing weight, ask yourself: is your regular approach to weight loss a form of insanity? Are you doing the same things over and over again and expecting a different result? Do you only connect weight loss with the food you eat? Have you been fighting the same battle of the same bulge with the same tools (i.e., crash diets, deprivation)? If you have, of course you will get the same results. Because if you are always dealing with the same questions, you will always get the same answers.

In the previous chapter, I wanted to help you familiarize yourself with some common relationships everyone has with food. Now I want you to take a look inside yourself. Ask yourself these questions – with honesty – even if nobody asks you. Because when you know yourself a little better, you will realize that the answer to long-lasting weight loss does not lie with the diet or the trainer, the answer ultimately lies with you.

Is Food Your Escape?

It doesn't matter who we are or what we do, we've all looked for life's rainbow at the end of a pot of malai kulfi. This test is not designed to understand whether you *sometimes* do this (because then we'd all qualify as emotional eaters). Rather, this set of questions has been designed to understand whether or not you have the tendency to use food as the *primary* way to cope with life's villains, vamps and heroes. Take this test to find out whether emotional eating is holding back your weight loss.

1. Is your hunger usually paired with an upsetting or joyous emotion?
   a. Mostly   b. Occasionally   c. Rarely

2. Do you crave a specific type of food (junk food/ fried foods/ sweets) when you are emotional?
   a. Mostly   b. Occasionally   c. Rarely

3. Does hunger come quickly and suddenly when you are feeling emotional?
   a. Mostly   b. Occasionally   c. Rarely

4. Do you notice a marked difference in your eating patterns between high-stress and no-stress situations?
   a. Mostly   b. Occasionally   c. Rarely

5. Do you feel that you are more in control of your emotions if you eat a chocolate or pastry or any other comfort food?
   a. Mostly   b. Occasionally   c. Rarely

6. Do you find yourself eating unconsciously?
   a. Mostly   b. Occasionally   c. Rarely

7. Do you continue to eat even after you're full just because it's available to you?
   a. Mostly   b. Occasionally   c. Rarely

8. Does your hunger feel urgent; if you don't get food, do you get cranky and panicky? (However, if you have diabetes, you don't need to answer this question.)
   a. Mostly   b. Occasionally   c. Rarely

9. Do you feel guilty about what/ how much you eat?
   a. Mostly   b. Occasionally   c. Rarely

10. Do you think of food so strongly that you can taste it?
    a. Mostly   b. Occasionally   c. Rarely

Mostly As (7 or more): You may have a tendency to eat in response to your feelings, especially when you are not hungry. More often than not, it is your emotions that dictate when and/ or how much you eat.

Mostly Bs (6–7 or more): While emotional triggers prompt you to eat, you do not always turn to food for comfort. You also use other ways to cope with stress or joy.

Mostly Cs (6–7 or more): Your emotions do not play much of a role in your food habits.

While life's ups and downs are inevitable, gaining weight doesn't have to be. What we need is a system of managing emotions that doesn't involve food. Think of anger or joy as being fluid, like water; it can be channelized any way you want. You can deal with it by going for a walk, venting with a friend, taking kickboxing or yoga classes – anything that suits your time and temperament. If you have scored 7 or more As on this test, make this a priority: find alternative outlets for your anger, pain, nervousness and other emotions. It is only when you know how to respond to your emotional cues that you can get moving towards the body you have always wanted.

THE 'TAKE FIVE' GUIDE TO EMOTIONAL EATING

When you feel the emotions pile on, or you feel you might give in to a binge you will later regret, take five, i.e., wait five minutes before you reach for that snack. Use this time to...

❏   *Get away.* Try to get out of the kitchen or the fridge and put some distance between you and the food. This will allow you to clear your head.

❏   *Get in touch.* Get in touch with your feelings. Ask yourself what's really going on. Are you angry? Nervous? Frustrated? Bored? It is only when you accept your feelings for what they are that you can find a way to cope with them.

❏   *Get real.* Tell yourself the ultimate truth about emotional eating. This is something we all know but only remember after the binge: you will almost always feel *worse* after eating, not better.

❏   *Get busy.* Five minutes will give you enough time to find a solution to your stress. Call a friend to vent or face your stress head on. If it's boredom that's prompting you to eat, then you need to immerse yourself in an activity to help you deal with it – go for a walk or catch a movie.

Are You Ready to Lose Weight?

This is probably the most 'unasked' question of all. Nobody ever asks you whether you are truly ready to lose weight. But what does this really mean?

When you get on a weight loss programme, you need to be prepared to make adjustments. You need to make space for your new lifestyle. Buying a weight loss book is one step. But it's like getting a haircut: just one step in a makeover. You might want to lose weight but is your body telling you one thing and your mind, another? Are you truly ready to make those adjustments? Are you prepared for the initial discomfort a new lifestyle will give you? Take this test and see where you are located on your weight loss journey.

IN THE LONG RUN

❏ *Face it.* Ultimately, no matter what you do, emotional eating is not coping with the situation, it's avoiding it. The situation that's causing you stress needs to be dealt with. Have a heart-to-heart with your boss, child, spouse, partner, mother-in-law or friend; find a way to confront or accept the stressful situation. It'll be a load off your mind – and your scale.

❏ *Write it down.* If emotional eating continually interferes with your efforts to lose weight, it might be a good idea to maintain a diary to record the emotional event that led to the binge, so that you remember what set you off and you are better prepared the next time.

❏ *Phone a friend.* Maintain a system for stress management. Keep handy a list of people you can call, or an activity you can organize for yourself at a moment's notice, so that you can immediately divert your attention.

❏ *Treat yourself.* Every time you succeed in avoiding a binge, reward yourself. Buy yourself something small and non-food related – like a dress or a book or a DVD – to celebrate. The more you ignore 'emotional' hunger, the better you will be at resisting it forever.

Glance at this checklist whenever you feel a binge coming on. Tick off the boxes as you go, and be prepared to say goodbye to emotional eating for good.

1. **Which of the following statements do you identify with the most?**
   a. I need to work harder and I can do much more.
   b. There is nothing I have not tried to lose weight.
   c. I'll lose weight at some point. What's the hurry?

2. **You realize you need to lose weight. What is your first reaction?**
   a. Hit the gym. NOW!
   b. I will start dieting next week, next month, whatever.
   c. More of me to love.

3. **How fast do you want to lose weight?**
   a. Gradually. I want to keep the weight off.

b. As soon as possible. I want results.

c. I haven't really thought about it.

4. **What kind of expectations do you have from a weight loss programme?**

a. I want to lose just enough weight in accordance with my height and age.

b. I want to look like Deepika Padukone or John Abraham.

c. I'm not sure right now but it's something I will do at some point in my life.

5. **How do you plan to prioritize time for exercise?**

a. I am ready to give up on going out with friends in order to go to the gym.

b. I don't know how much time I can set aside for exercising.

c. Exercise? Can't I just diet? I don't have time to work out.

6. **On a scale of 1 to 10, 10 being the highest, how important is reaching your goal weight to you?**

a. 8 to 10

b. 5 to 7

c. 0 to 3

7. **How do you see this book?**

a. As a way to start the process of weight loss.

b. Let's see if it tells me stuff I already know.

c. I just wanted something to read and this book happened to be around.

8. **How do you think you can lose weight?**

a. Healthy lifestyle.

b. Crash diet.

c. It will happen when it has to happen.

Mostly As (6 or more): You're in the weight loss zone! Your motivation levels are high and you are geared to lose weight the healthy way. You're not willing to compromise on the means to lose weight and want long-lasting results.

Mostly Bs (6 or more): You're motivated but you also look for shortcuts. This may result in your being impulsive, starting off your journey with excitement but losing interest midway. Frustrations may also set in if you don't see results soon, ultimately making you give up before you reach your goal.

Mostly Cs (6 or more): You may not be ready to make a proper commitment to a weight loss programme.

If you didn't score well on this test, don't lose heart. I've seen clients get on their weight loss programme half-heartedly, but as they get leaner, they get keener, which helps them reach their goal weight faster. If you have mostly scored Cs, try these tips to enhance your motivational levels:

LIST

List all your reasons for wanting to lose weight or stay healthy and slim. Add more reasons to your list as you think of them. Read this list every day (maybe while you brush your teeth or sip your morning tea). It will only take you five minutes to prepare and barely a minute to read. You will be surprised at how motivating this is.

VISUALIZE

Visualization is an extremely powerful, proven tool for weight management. It is a mental technique that enables you to imagine that you have already achieved your goal. It is used by athletes, CEOs and other successful people all over the world to achieve both personal and professional dreams. The idea behind this technique is that thoughts become things.

Visualize yourself at your goal weight. You're wearing that one dress or bikini or your wedding lehenga or that sharp double-breasted suit you have always wanted to wear. Imagine yourself stepping into a wedding or party. Picture how people will look at you, think of the compliments you will receive. Imagine how much lighter you will be feeling, how much faster you will be walking about. Focus on the reactions of those who have always made fun of your weight. And how their jaws drop as they see the new you.

While I've given you an example to get you started, we will be going deeper into the process in the next section, where I want you to create your own weight loss vision. It's incredibly useful in getting you all fired up to start losing weight. And it is mind-numbingly effective in helping you reach your goal weight.

GET INSPIRED

Pick up a magazine or go online and cut out or download inspirational stories of people who have succeeded in losing weight. People who lose weight are not superhuman. They just decided to go for it! If they can do it, so can you.

MIND IT

Use your subconscious to help you lose weight. It's a lot easier if your mind is on your side! Motivational tapes and hypnosis help your brain absorb the right messages and help you to relax. You have nothing to lose by trying it out.

Is Food Your Boss?

Does food determine who you are and what you do? The reason why weight gain forms a recurring pattern in your life might be because food controls you more than you realize. If you are obsessed with the idea of food, or if you think it occupies more space in your life than it should, take this test to see if you have a tendency to be addicted to the food you eat.

1. Do you obsess over thoughts of food?

    ☐ Yes   ☐ No

2. Do you consume large quantities of food to the point that you feel sick?

    ☐ Yes   ☐ No

3. Do you feel anxious while or after eating, which leads to further eating?

    ☐ Yes   ☐ No

4. Do you tend to eat on the sly or when you are alone?

    ☐ Yes   ☐ No

5. Do you tend to hide food when you see someone approaching?

    ☐ Yes   ☐ No

6. Would you rather eat your favourite food than socialize?

    ☐ Yes   ☐ No

7. Do you go on eating binges a couple of times a week or more?

    ☐ Yes   ☐ No

8. Do you tend to hide your favourite food in your room or cupboard so that nobody finds it?

    ☐ Yes   ☐ No

9. Do you lack self-control while eating?

    ☐ Yes   ☐ No

10 Do you tend to overeat when the food is in front of you?

    ☐ Yes   ☐ No

Mostly Yes (7 or more): If you have answered yes to most of the above, you *may* have a strong tendency to eat compulsively and are prone to harmful eating.

Sometimes Yes, Sometimes No (5–6): While food is important to you, it is far easier for you to say no to food, so all you need to do is make a few adjustments to your eating habits.

Mostly No (7 or more): This suggests you eat to live, not live to eat, and food does not take priority over other things in your life.

If you scored more than 7 yesses on this test, relax. Help is at hand.

The intention of this test is to check your *tendency* towards compulsive eating and bingeing. If you have scored 7 or more yesses, it means that while you are definitely prone to harmful eating, you may or may not be addicted to food.

Now, this is where you need to be honest with yourself. If you got a high score on this test, it might explain why you aren't able to lose the weight and keep it off. Because no matter how much you try to diet or exercise, your compulsive need to eat will stop you from reaching your goal weight.

So what now?

Treat your high score as a warning sign. Check yourself, alert your friends and family, see if you can learn to control your eating habits. And if you honestly think it's beyond you, seek professional help. Maybe you – and people around you – have blamed you for your lack of willpower when, in actual fact, you have a condition that needs help. Don't panic, but please don't ignore the symptoms. Help is at hand, and this problem has many tried-and-tested solutions suited to your convenience.

Are You Losing Weight for YOU?

No one can tell you to lose weight. Your husband, mother, doctor and even your genes can do or say what they want but weight loss is one of the most intensely personal decisions you will ever make.

It is a choice that is always yours and yours alone. Your body, your choice. I believe that if you are losing weight for reasons other than that you truly, madly want to, the results will be short-lived and frustrating. And maybe the reason you haven't been losing weight is because you have been doing it for someone – or something – else.

your body, your choice

1. **When you find out that you have put on a few kilos, which of these statements do you identify with the most?**
   a. I must start exercising today!
   b. I'll go on a diet next month.
   c. It's only a few kilos, not 10, right? What's the fuss about?

2. **Weight loss to you is**
   a. More about how you look.
   b. More about how you feel.
   c. More about trying to impress or please other people.

3. **In the past, when it came to joining a gym or starting a weight loss plan:**
   a. It has been entirely your own decision to lose weight.
   b. Loved ones/ doctors/ people around you partly influenced your decision to lose weight.
   c. Loved ones/ doctors/ people around you strongly influenced your decision to lose weight.

4. **Why do you want to lose weight?**
   a. To look and feel good.
   b. To be fit.
   c. Because my family/ husband/ wife is forcing me to.

5. **You've just discovered that you've gained weight. How do you feel about it?**
   a. I'm really upset. It's the single most important thing which is affecting my confidence and mood.
   b. I'm a little upset. It bothers me a bit.
   c. It makes no difference to me.

6. **Imagine that you have reached your goal weight. Which of the following statements do you identify with the most?**
   a. I have achieved one of my dreams!
   b. Okay, now what?
   c. Finally! Now my family will get off my back. I'm free!

7. **Being in shape is**
   a. Loving myself and my body.
   b. Important but not fully in my control.
   c. I am in shape. Round is a shape.

8. **How do you react when someone says, 'Oh, you have put on weight since I saw you last.'?**
   a. You agree. And then go straight to the gym.
   b. You agree. And then go straight home and drown your sorrow in chocolate.
   c. You disagree. You make excuses, get defensive or tell him/ her, 'You're no supermodel either.'

9. **If your close friend or relative suggests you go to a fabulous nutritionist or join a gym that has done wonders for many**
   a. You take the number and make an appointment immediately.
   b. Your mother/ spouse takes the number and you say you will call later.
   c. Your mother/ spouse makes the appointment and you go along to please them.

Mostly As (7 or more): You believe you have a weight problem and are convinced that you need to take the appropriate steps to ensure you lose weight.

Mostly Bs (6–7): You are aware but not fully convinced or motivated to lose weight.

Mostly Cs (6–7): You are in denial of your weight gain and don't think you have a problem. Weight loss is something you embark on to make other people happy.

If you're losing weight for someone else, whether it's someone you're attracted to or someone who loves you, your weight loss is centred around what that person wants. Your levels of motivation depend on the nature of your relationship with that person and could fluctuate, because you're not losing weight for yourself.

When it comes down to it, it's *your* body. It doesn't matter what anyone else says, thinks or does. There will always be someone who thinks you need to be thinner or better dressed, but that's their opinion – you can take it or leave it. Focus on your goals and your body because it's your choice to work out.

Weight loss will help *you* be healthier, it will keep *your* sugar levels down, it will prevent *your* heart from disease, it will help *you* run up the stairs without getting breathless. The benefits are yours, the pleasure is yours and the success will only be yours!

Use the motivational tips listed in 'Are You Ready to Lose Weight?' on page 35 to kick your weight loss into high gear. You will only effectively lose – and maintain the weight you have lost – if you remember the most important element of any weight loss programme: you.

Do You Want to Be a Thinner Version of You or Someone Else?

In other words, do you love you?

Ahh, this is a biggie. I cannot tell you how many clients walk in with the expectation that my weight loss programme will make them look like supermodels. This question ties in with how much you love yourself and your body. If you want to change the body you see in the mirror, you have to first embrace the shape and features that make you unique. If you don't, you will never be happy with the end result.

1. Do you worry excessively about your looks and constantly compare yourself with a friend, family member or an actor?

   ☐ Yes   ☐ No

2. Do you feel enamoured by certain celebrities and feel that if you worked hard to look like them, you actually can?

   ☐ Yes   ☐ No

3. Do you check how you look in mirrors or other reflecting objects (i.e., windows, car bumpers, spoons, etc) at every opportunity possible?

   ☐ Yes   ☐ No

4. Do you get easily influenced by beauty commercials or want to do things like plastic surgery or dermatological procedures (i.e., Botox) in order to look like someone you idolize?

   ☐ Yes   ☐ No

5. Do you think you are unattractive to the extent that you go to great lengths to camouflage your perceived flaw/s (i.e., wear baggy clothing, extremely heavy make-up or maintain a specific body posture or angle while taking photographs)?

   ☐ Yes   ☐ No

6. Do you tend to avoid certain places and/ or activities (i.e., parties, dating, swimming, restaurants, theatres, etc) because you don't want others to see your flaws?

   ☐ Yes   ☐ No

7. Do you feel uncomfortable when looking at your reflection or photographs and try to avoid having your picture taken?

   ☐ Yes   ☐ No

8. Do you compulsively seek information relating to the diet and exercise regimes of celebrities or people whose bodies you admire?

   ☐ Yes   ☐ No

9. Do you often seek reassurance from loved ones about your looks and doubt them even if they give a positive reply?

☐ Yes   ☐ No

10. Do you feel dissatisfied no matter how much weight you have lost?

☐ Yes   ☐ No

Mostly Yes (7 or more): You are not happy with the way you look and think you are excessively flawed. The flaws are more in your mind than in your body. You have unrealistic expectations about the results, which causes you distress. This could lead to you developing an unhealthy relationship with both food and weight loss.

Both Yes and No (5–6): You may have concerns about your outward appearance and are preoccupied with perceived flaws, which may be unrealistic or unhealthy but can be managed. Catch it now.

Mostly No (7 or more): You appreciate the way you look and have good, well-developed self-esteem.

Anamika was a pretty girl, an aspiring engineer who had Polycystic Ovarian Syndrome or PCOS. She was dedicated to her meal plan, wrote in her diary every day and worked out regularly. She dropped a massive 30 kilos on my programme. But the more weight she lost, the unhappier she felt. Why? Because she didn't look like Deepika Padukone. Her mother was distressed, naturally, as was I. She lost all that weight and she wasn't even able to enjoy the fruits of her labour.

This is one of the most important lessons you can learn. Love yourself. I cannot emphasize this enough. Because, as the weight goes down and the inches start coming off, you are far less likely to continue the programme if you think you aren't matching up to the picture in your head. If you have an unhealthy obsession with an unrealistic ideal, you may want to talk to someone qualified to understand whether you are suffering from low self-esteem, which has been the trigger for so many cases of eating disorders.

Please remember that whether they are actors, models or sports stars, they are getting the best out of the bodies they have been given. All they are doing is maximizing their own potential. Your body is unique, your body is yours. Appreciate every feature, wrinkle and line – it is God's gift to you. Enjoy it, revel in it and be the best you can be.

MIND OVER PLATTER

The Decisions You Make at the Top Affect Your Bottom

Your brain is a beautiful thing. It is the headquarters of your entire decision-making process. It tells you to say yes to a first date, to agree with your boss even when he's wrong, or makes you buy that toy for your son even though you know he will forget about it by the end of the week.

But if your brain can say yes, it can also say no.

Your brain will tell you to walk over the crack in the pavement or avoid taking the dark alley on your way home. It can make you end the call with the annoying call-centre executive or say no when your sabziwala charges you too much. In short, there is nothing your body can do without your mind knowing.

When it comes down to it, losing weight is all about making decisions. Saying no to the things that won't help us lose weight and saying yes to the things that will. But we already know this. We know better than to tear into that pizza an hour before dinner or take a second helping of cheesecake. Sure, the brain responds to hunger pangs and signals from our body. But we eat even when our body isn't asking for food. The point I am trying to make is that the same brain that causes you to make unhealthy decisions can also enable you to make healthy ones.

If the human brain is as open to saying no as it is to saying yes, why do we treat willpower like it's this magical quality God has bestowed upon a chosen few? Why do we accept our weight gain with the stubborn belief that we do not have the ability to lose weight?

What if I told you that willpower could be taught? That the key to long-lasting weight loss is nothing but developing the habit of saying no. What if I said you can 'learn' to lose weight? What if I told you that you can reach a stage where making healthy choices becomes as instinctive – and as easy – as brushing your teeth? And all that stands between you and the body you have always wanted is one word – no, not diet or starvation or denial – but simply PRACTICE.

How do we make healthy habits? And what stands in our way? I have worked with Dr Anjali Chhabria and her team of psychologists at Mindtemple to help you understand not only how the human brain forms habits, but how you can form new habits. We have developed mental toolkits so that before you decide what to eat and how to eat it, you know how to get battle-ready on the most important battleground of them all – your mind.

The Mind

Understanding Willpower

'I Want to Lose Weight but I Don't Have the Willpower'

If you think willpower is like a red-carpet event that admits only a select few, you couldn't be more wrong. Willpower is like love, compassion or wisdom. We all have it. Everyone's invited. Before you throw your hands up in the air and simply give up on your body, ask yourself this:

❏ How long did it take you to drive a car?
❏ How long did it take you to ride a bicycle?
❏ How long did it take you to master a new gadget?

Remember when you got your first cell-phone? Sending SMSes were a pain in the neck, right? You typed slowly, got half the spellings wrong, and became best friends with the delete button. After a week or two, it was a whole lot easier. Today you can SMS in your sleep.

For the most part, willpower is a skill. It has to be strengthened. You have to keep practising. With every no you say to that gulab jamun, it becomes easier to say no the second time around. Or the fourth. The more you say yes to the pakodas being passed around, the harder it'll be to say no the next time. It's as simple as that.

But if It's so Simple, Why Is It so Hard?

To answer this question we must first understand how the human brain forms a habit. Habits start off as thoughts in your mind. These thoughts set off a chain reaction within your body, which leads you to act on that thought. And what provides you with the ability to translate thoughts into action? That job is done with the help of nerve cells in your body, also called neurons.

Here's how it works: If you're looking at chocolate mousse for the first time in your life and are thinking about eating it, the neurons in your brain send information to the neurons in your spinal cord which in turn send information to the neurons in your hand, which takes a spoonful and puts it in your mouth.

From the moment you think of it to the moment you physically pick up the food and eat it, this chain of neurons works to translate your thought into action. This chain of neurons is called a neural pathway and right from opening the door to typing on your keyboard, every action you perform has a neural pathway of its own.

If you give in to the temptation of eating chocolate mousse the first time you see it, it establishes a weak neural pathway. But if you eat chocolate mousse every time you see it, the neural pathway gets stronger. With enough repetitions, eating chocolate mousse at sight becomes more and more 'automatic' and a habit is born. In other words, you develop a habit when the same neural pathway is used over and over again. In some cases, it takes just 10 days to form a habit;[4] in other cases it takes longer.

Whether it's skipping breakfast or eating dessert after every meal, when you've formed a habit that has made you 10, 20 or 30 kilos overweight, you have developed a strong neural pathway.

---

[4] 'How Do I Form a Good Habit?', http://ergonomics.about.com/od/ergonomicbasics/f/form_good_habit.htm, accessed on 10/1/12

Now, imagine a weak neural pathway as a piece of string and a strong neural pathway as a piece of rope – which one is easier to 'break'?* In other words, just as your mother told you, old habits die hard. That's why it can sometimes be hard for us to build our willpower.

But you're in luck. Good habits or bad ones, your brain is wired to make new habits all the time! The brain *wants* to make habits because any habit is 'automatic' behaviour. And automatic behaviour allows the brain to pay attention to more complex functions. So, whether you like it or not, when you repeat the same behaviour often enough, it becomes part of you. Can you imagine a life where your healthy habits are hard to break? Stay healthy long enough, and you won't have to imagine any more.

The Diet Mentality

On the diet. Off the diet. On the diet. Off the diet. Switch on. Switch off. You don't yo-yo because you 'can't' lose weight, or because something is 'wrong' with the diet (a lot of fad diets are genuinely harmful, but I'm referring to a balanced diet here). You yo-yo because you believe that the weight you have lost is permanent.

It's not. No weight loss is.

Always remember that whichever weight you are at, you are doing something to maintain it. If you're a woman, at 5 feet 2 inches and weigh 100 kilos, there are reasons for it. You are eating x number of calories, you're not exercising – you are doing something to maintain your 100 kilos. If you've now lost 40 kilos, you can't eat the same way you used to, still not exercise, and expect *not* to gain the weight back. Bottom line:

If you have a new body, you can't do old things to maintain it.

* You cannot actually break the neural pathway – only weaken it.

I'm not saying you should banish all your favourite foods forever. I'm simply saying there are certain things you have to do during your weight loss phase. My maintenance plan will not allow you to pass up high-calorie foods. Whatever you want to eat can be re-integrated into your system when you have lost the weight you wanted to. Long-term weight loss is about balance, proportion and control. So that you can call on your favourite foods when you want to. Not because you *need* to.

When you change the way you eat, you bid goodbye to a lifetime of yo-yo journeys filled with false starts. Don't you want it to be over for once and for all? Don't you want to spend your life focusing on other things? Think of a lifestyle change as the last ever weight loss programme you will be on. The last start you will ever make.

Developing Willpower

So how do you get your hot new body? You move your head to one side. Then move it to the other. Shake vigorously. Repeat.

In other words, you just say NO. Again and again and again.

Closing the door on the old you is a little hard in the beginning. Developing willpower is like trying on a pair of jeans that are a few sizes too small for you. You can't try it on and see if it fits you. You need to slowly fit into it. You're going to be up against all sorts of barriers, temptations and mindsets. Your job, therefore, is to plan ahead and reduce the obstacles you might encounter.

When you're in the safety of your home, and the junk food is locked away and you're eating the healthy, nutritious meal in front of you, you don't think about how strong or weak your willpower is. But when your neighbour suddenly comes over with a dish of homemade mithai or a friend insists you come over for a heavy dinner, that's when your willpower is tested.

Say you're at a party on the first day of your new lifestyle. You've stuck to the plan and you've eaten healthy throughout the evening. You're just about to leave when the host comes to you with a silver tray with a huge, fat, luscious serving of

ice-cream

Just when you thought you had sorted it out, the war starts in your head again.

The old you is shouting at the top of its lungs:
EAT IT! JUST TAKE A BITE! YOU'VE WORKED SO HARD!

The new you is small and powerless next to it:
Hey, don't do that. You're nearly there.

In the beginning, the old you will keep pulling you back like a rubberband, desperately trying to bully you into winning the war. But by ignoring it – like you would a child throwing a tantrum – in a matter of weeks, its voice will come down to a whisper. The same situation will then play itself out like this:

Old you: Maybe I could have a tiny bite.

New you: THANKS, BUT I DON'T FEEL LIKE IT RIGHT NOW. MAYBE NEXT TIME?

Isn't the human body fantastic?

BOOST YOUR WILLPOWER

Need help with boosting your willpower? Eat right and eat more frequently. To understand why this is important is to understand how digestion works. The end product of every little thing you consume – be it mango lassi or a piece of apple – is eventually glucose, i.e., sugar. To ensure that you don't keep giving in to your cravings, keep your sugar levels stable through the day. And you can only do that by eating healthy and eating more often (every two hours).

Here's why. When you're eating the right things and eating at smaller intervals, there is a sustained release of energy in your body through the day and your sugar levels are stable. But if you wait too long before eating or eat foods that get converted into glucose too fast (sugary foods like cakes and mithai), your sugar levels spike when you eat that particular food (leading to a burst of energy) and then crash, leaving you with a tired, sluggish body that craves more sugar. You then eat as a 'pick me up', which weakens your ability to resist unhealthy foods for your next meal. It's a vicious cycle.

Eat right. Eat frequently. While we will go into this in more detail later, this simple principle is an extremely important part of your weight loss phase. And beyond.

'BUT IT'S JUST ONE BITE'

It's not like you *can't* have ice-cream or chocolate during your weight loss phase. It's just that going off your healthy meal plan too early in the game weakens your ability to resist temptation in the future. Like a marathon runner, you have to train your muscles first and then take rest days.[5] You can't take rest days *before* you've trained your muscles. You have to build up that resistance so that when you do give in to your favourite foods, you are confident that you have now developed the 'skill' to resist.

It takes about 20 minutes for your stomach to send the signal to your brain that you are full. But 20 minutes can feel like 20 hours if you are trying to train yourself to eat healthy, and you can make many decisions in these 20 minutes that can really set back your

[5] Judith Beck, *The Beck DIET Solution*, Oxmoor House, 2008

efforts. I've devised a three-step plan to help you develop your willpower. While you can come up with your own plan to make sure you keep saying NO till it becomes a habit, you could use this to help you get started.

LEVEL 1 | Control Your Food Environment

The start of your weight loss programme is when you are the most vulnerable. You're a newbie at this stage, trying to change age-old habits. You may or may not have the strength to compete with the big boys. Can you start off with 40 surya namaskars on the second day of your yoga class? No, right? So you need some help in resisting temptation by consciously controlling your external environment.

My clients sometimes start their weight loss programme during wedding season, or during a really hectic time at work. While there is never a bad time to start getting healthy, it'll be harder to stick to your plan if you expose yourself to temptation too early.

And yet, this is it. The success at Level 1 dictates how well you do for the rest of your weight loss programme. This is the stage where you are weakening old neural pathways while simultaneously making and strengthening new ones. This is the stage where you will be confronting habits that have led you to be 10 or 20 or 40 kilos overweight. This is the stage where you will snap at your spouse or friends, feel like life's hit rock bottom, act irritable, cranky or depressed and hate everything and everyone around you. This is when you will probably be obsessed with thoughts of the food you cannot have, as opposed to the food you *can*. You will probably 'fail' once, twice, three times or more. If you fail a fourth time, you will convince yourself that you can't do it.

I like to call this the storm before the calm.

Ride out the storm. Keep telling yourself that this is the worst it will get. Be prepared. Be alert. Take out your raincoat (healthy food), stay away from the rain (temptations) until you see the clouds clear up. Forgive yourself if you get a little drenched now and then, but make sure you return to your new lifestyle. You can go out for good when the sun's out. And trust me, you will know when the coast is clear.

How to Control Your Food Environment

No one's a (thousand) island

Accept that you cannot do this alone. Get friends, family or co-workers to pitch in with your weight loss efforts for the first few weeks. Ask them to help you kick junk food out of your house, not order in fattening food (or at least not force you to join them) and make sure you have access to healthy meals. Appoint one person to be your 'conscience', and call him/ her whenever you feel the urge to go off your meal plan. Assure the people you recruit in this effort that they have to be vigilant with you for only a short time.

Food is NOT entertainment

Savour this little nugget of information as you plan your social life in the first few weeks of your new meal plan. Don't consciously make plans revolving around food at this early stage. Stick to movies, plays and anything that doesn't involve food (or goes beyond tea and coffee) or refer to the list of food-free activities in the first chapter.

Reward yourself with everything but food

Whenever you successfully escape an emotional eating session or combat the urge to binge, reward yourself. One client loved fancy stationary (stickers, high-end glossy notebooks, fancy ink pens) and she would buy herself something small each time she avoided a binge, or when she did well for the day or week. Pick your own reward cycle, whether it's a massage or a pedicure, and treat yourself when the going gets good. But don't get too used to it. Once your system become comfortable with healthy food, your need to reward yourself will grow less, and then disappear altogether.

Get back in the saddle as soon as possible

If you get off your healthy meal plan, don't make yourself feel miserable or immerse yourself in guilt-ridden bingeing or 'compensate' by over-exercising or starving yourself the next day. Don't blame yourself. Blame a stubborn neural pathway instead. Get back on the programme as fast as you got off it. And forgive yourself. It happens.

Be organized

Be prepared with healthy snacks/ fillers (I've given you a list of these later in the book) and carry them with you on the go. If you work at an office, carry your lunch with you, plan your healthy meals for the day in advance. Make sure the right food is available to you when you need it, because your body will not be able to make the right choices if it is left to feel hungry at this early stage.

Hang on

The simplest advice is the best. Hang on. Because it only gets better from here.

LEVEL 2 | Testing One, Two, Three

Three weeks down the line, you're already feeling better. Your clothes are looser; you have more energy. This is when you slowly enter temptation-filled environments and test your ability to resist. You can probably sit through coffee sessions without ordering the dessert of the day, or go for a movie and buy a healthy snack or drink. There will be days when it will be hard to say no, but you will have the confidence that you can get back on track faster, because your resistance is much stronger than when you started out.

LEVEL 3 | I'm in Charge

Now you can sit at dinner comfortably and order healthy while the rest of your friends are eating fried cheese. You don't need to lock away your snacks any more. You make healthy choices. If you do give in, it will be occasional. This is the phase you will be in for the rest of your life, where you maintain a balance between healthy and unhealthy.

Many studies have concluded that the human brain takes 21 to 28 days to change a habit. So you could reach Level 3 in less than a month! Results vary, but I have many clients who have achieved this successfully within this timeframe.

Losing weight is a waiting game. That's all it is. That's the big secret. You just have to play the game. You have to forcibly propel your body into that lifestyle and *wait*. It's going be overwhelming but within, you will feel better, fitter, stronger and won't want to go back. Soon it'll be harder and harder to live with the foods you thought you couldn't live without. Isn't it worth investing a few weeks of hardship so you can be free for the rest of your life? Think about it.

losing **weight** is a **waiting** game

Life After Saying No: When It Stops Feeling Like a Battle

I believe the reason so many of us give up so early in our weight loss journey is because when we start off, the battle of the bulge literally feels like a battle. It's such a struggle to make new habits, we think we will keep feeling this way. We think we will always be upset, depressed, irritable and wondering if it's worth it. We think we will always be the person who never gets to 'have fun' and we may want to stop our weight loss journey because we 'just want to enjoy life'. Always remember that the fight between the old you and the new you is simply a fight to change behaviours that have shaped your body for years, even decades.

Of course it's not going to be easy at first. But there's a light at the end of the tunnel. And it's bright, beautiful and lasts forever.

The sweet truth is that your body gets used to healthy foods faster than you think. When you've eaten healthy and smart for long enough (and I'm talking weeks, not years), the food you lusted after so desperately fails to interest you. Your tastes change. Can you imagine ordering a healthy salad because you *want* to (since greasy food now makes you feel nauseous)? Can you imagine drinking tea without sugar because otherwise it tastes too sweet? Yes, the human body is *that* adaptive.

Clients who lost weight on my programme told me that when they ate a lot of high-cal food after a long break, they felt uneasy and sick. And it's easy to understand why. When they suddenly overloaded their stomachs with huge quantities of food, they forced their digestive systems to pump more enzymes, digestive juices and speed up the absorption process. After a long break from unhealthy eating, their bodies went through a lot of turmoil to digest that food. No wonder they felt tired, sluggish, nauseous and low on energy.

Make a fist. Now open up your palm about 50 per cent. That's the size of your stomach. Depending on how much you feed it, it can, over time, expand to the size of a football. Eat smart, and your stomach reverts to its normal size. Simply, the stomach has a size zero of its own. And no human body *needs* more food than that.

the stomach has a size zero of its own

When you start saying no, you will struggle to enforce these new choices on your old body. But when you have a new body, you will struggle with enforcing your old choices on it. Eating lots of unhealthy food will no longer be your decision to make. Because your body will protest before you do.

Welcome to your new life.

The Mindsets
or
What Stands in Our Way

- ❏ *Divide.* Start by breaking up your goal into smaller, bite-sized pieces. If your aim is to be thinner, and not thin, you will always achieve your goal, no matter how much weight you lose. If you have 30 kilos to lose, aim to lose it at intervals of 5 kilos each.

- ❏ *Feel.* Every time the scale goes down, pick up an equivalent weight and carry it around your house to enjoy yourself at your new weight. When Oprah Winfrey lost 67 pounds, she famously wheeled in 67 pounds of actual fat on her show to give her audience an idea of how much weight she had lost. You can do the same thing. If you've lost a kilo, just take a kilo of fruit, vegetables or any object of equivalent weight and feel it in your hand. It probably feels heavier than you imagined, and soon you have to put it down because your hand can't take the weight. That's how much weight you've lost! Imagine doing that with 5 kilos. And if you've lost 10 kilos, it won't even be easy to pick the weight up!

- ❏ *Imagine.* You have a pair of blue jeans you have been struggling to get into ever since you went on that vacation. You pull them out of the cupboard. Before you lost 3 kilos, they wouldn't even go up. But now, if you suck your tummy in, you might be able to button up. Have you lost all the weight you wanted to? No. But can you do things you weren't able to do before? Absolutely.

- ❏ *Celebrate.* Every time the scale goes down, treat yourself in non-food ways. Get a massage, a fancy pedicure, go shopping (you might be able to buy a smaller dress size!), enjoy a movie. You're special. You're losing the weight, so let's celebrate!

Some of my clients have been so happy with the way they look and feel *before* they achieve their goal that they have *changed* their goal and reset their target to a higher weight. The moment you get into the Thinner and not Thin Mindset, that's when you know you're treating your body with the love and encouragement it deserves.

2. THE ALL OR NOTHING MINDSET

It usually starts with one piece of chocolate. Or a handful of chips. And ends with four ice-creams, three sodas, four packets of peanuts and a mountain of fries. 'All or Nothing' is a classic mindset which derails your weight loss efforts more frequently than you think. Ironically, it is a mindset born out of wanting to be perfect, where dieters seek perfection in both following the diet, and in *not* following it. Welcome to the land of 'No Half-measure'.

Why do we do it? Well, there are a number of reasons: the feeling that since we have 'broken' the diet, we might as well start again tomorrow; or if we eat whatever we want on that day, and that day alone, 'it doesn't count'. Well, unfortunately, it does count. Every little thing you eat counts. And every little thing you don't eat counts as well.

Imagine you have a beautiful set of six bone-china teacups. These teacups are in ivory, very delicate, patterned with birds and flowers. You take the set out when you have some special guests over. You're about to start pouring the tea and… Oh, no! Your best friend from school knocks one over and shatters the cup. Your heart sinks (you knew you should have given her a plastic cup: she's so clumsy!). What do you do? Would you:

1. Break the other five teacups? You might as well, since the set has been ruined.
2. Be extremely careful with the rest, and ensure that the remaining five are preserved?
3. Throw your friend out of the house?

The 'All or Nothing' approach to weight loss is like breaking all six teacups because you broke one. And not salvaging your effort when you can. I only use the teacup example to highlight the fact that you needn't add on 3000 extra calories because you've added 500 more than you had planned. The food won't even taste as good.

☐ **IS THIS YOU?** *(Tick this box if this is how you see weight loss)*

VERSUS

THE TEACUP MINDSET

You're human. No one can be perfectly healthy day after day after day. I can't, my clients can't. You may break one teacup by accident. But you will always break the rest deliberately.

❏ *Stop.* Like in emotional eating, stop yourself before it becomes a binge you will regret. Put some distance between yourself and the food. Get out of the house, call a friend to chat, or do something to distract yourself.

❏ *Write.* It may not be easy at first but do write down your thoughts when you are making an 'All or Nothing' decision. Note the times you give in to a binge, and note the times you stick to your plan. The more often you arrest a binge, the better you become at resisting it in future.

❏ *Celebrate.* Celebrate every time you prevent an 'All or Nothing' decision: get a massage or go shopping and buy yourself something nice. Revel in the feeling of being in control.

You have to remind yourself that this is not a diet – this is a food plan where, eventually, everything will be allowed. 'All or Nothing' comes from a mentality of being on a 'diet'. Move away from the idea of a diet – that's when you lose the 'All or Nothing' Mindset.

3. THE LUXURY MINDSET

There are many who think of weight loss as a luxury – like an exotic vacation; something that can be done when resources like time and money are available. This is because many associate weight gain with looks and not with health. I believe this mindset can put the brakes on any good intention to get back in shape because when you look at it as cosmetic, it invariably scores lower than work, kids, parents, friends, entertainment or travel. Weight loss then ties in with weddings or parties or how you want to look in a bikini. And who has the time for vanity when you have screaming deadlines or personal dramas?

☐   **IS THIS YOU?** (*Tick this box if this is how you see weight loss*)

VERSUS

THE EMERGENCY MINDSET

More often than not, we only react to what we immediately see. We can immediately see tyres and love handles. We can immediately see chunky calves and paunches. What we cannot see is the havoc poor eating wreaks on our organs and systems. We only see it when we start to feel it. By then it is probably too late to do anything about it. We can cure, yes, but we have lost the golden opportunity to prevent.

Think of the link between weight gain and disease in terms of a typical Bollywood movie scene. The hero and heroine – after discovering that they love each other – are running towards each other in slow motion on a beach/ in a garden/ at the airport. After what seems an eternity, they meet each other halfway and hug, kiss or whatever the censor board allows that year. Now replace the hero with weight gain and the heroine with disease (diabetes, heart disease, take your pick). They *will* meet at some point. It's inevitable. Weight gain is nothing but disease in slow motion.*

The difference between my clients who have medical conditions and those who don't is the sense of urgency. Those whose doctors have pushed them into the nutritionist's consulting room bring with them serious medical reports, matching expressions, and the feeling that they have to do something *now*.

If you had diabetes or a heart problem, wouldn't you be forced to take care of your body differently? You would automatically watch your sugar levels and fat intake and exercise because you didn't have a choice, right? Take weight loss seriously. Treat it as an emergency before it becomes one. I don't mean to alarm you, but I do want you to realize that while weight gain may or may not be about the way you look, it is always, always about the way you feel.

4. THE 'WILL IT HAPPEN?' MINDSET

They came, they lost, they disappeared. And all because they didn't trust their bodies.

The sudden change from unhealthy to healthy has shown fantastic results on some of my clients, who lose 5 kilos in the first month itself. They lose fast because they are eating healthy and at higher frequencies – something they have never done in their life, and which positively impacts their weight loss. But as the body settles into the new regime, weight loss is slower and usually never replicates the success of the initial months. Instead of losing 5 kilos, they may lose at the medically recommended rate of 2 or 3 kilos per month. Clients get discouraged with their slower results and when the weight doesn't disappear quickly every month, they do.

The 'Will It Happen?' Mindset is a mind plagued by doubt, where you do all the right things at the right pace but still do not

---

* Other pre-existing causes notwithstanding

believe that you will get results. I believe it to be a matter of trust, where you simply lack faith in your body and in yourself, and you wonder if you will ever reach your goal weight. The influence of this mindset is strong enough not only to convince you to abort your attempts to lose weight but also to make you believe that you just don't have what it takes to be thinner in the future. Because you question your body instead of simply taking your body's ability to lose weight for granted.

☐   **IS THIS YOU?** *(Tick this box if this is how you see weight loss)*

VERSUS

THE 'IT WILL HAPPEN' MINDSET

Vishal weighed in at 116 kilos when he walked into my clinic for the first time. He had everything going for him. He was an MBA graduate from one of the world's most prestigious business schools, worked with a premier consultancy firm, was a gold medallist in economics and was fun and outgoing. He was all this but he couldn't walk up a flight of stairs without feeling like he had climbed Mount Everest. He was only 34 years old.

I put him on meal plans that included rice, potatoes, bread and a lot of his favourite foods. He breezed through the first 20 kilos and then reached a plateau. For four months. He was depressed with his efforts, and it was harder and harder for him to stay focused. He brought both his weight loss diary and his grumpiness when he came to see me. But he came for his appointments on time. He exercised. And he ate healthy. Suddenly, the weight just started coming off kilo by kilo. It took him time but he eventually reached his goal weight because he did the one thing many of us forget about – he trusted his body.

When you invest in the stock market, you aren't always sure that you will make money. There is no such thing as a guaranteed return, even blue chip stocks have been known to make you suffer. But invest in your body and you will always win.

When you're doing the right things, and eating the right way, reaching your goal weight is just a matter of time. You will reach plateaus, and you will find yourself faced with the difficult decision to stay or to give up. Always stay. If you're fulfilling your end of the deal by doing the right things, your body will always pay you back. And how.

5. THE 'I DON'T HAVE TIME' MINDSET

'Eat smaller meals frequently? Low oil? Carry food from home? Pooja, come on! I'm in meetings through the day, I have a kid, I have a demanding mother-in-law, how can I take care of this too?'

When people say they don't want to make time for themselves or they really don't have the time, I think it's nothing but a tried-and-tested excuse. At the end of the day, you still have to eat. If you're saying you don't have time you are basically saying you don't want to make any changes but you still want to lose weight.

Unfortunately, that isn't possible. A new lifestyle needs two things from you – a little bit of your time and a little bit of space. It needs physical time in that you need to exercise (and cook or shop, if you do it for yourself) and space in your mind (where you need to keep thinking about how to make healthy decisions). But you will only feel conscious of it until you get used to your new lifestyle. Your body needs your full cooperation. It needs you to invest in it. The question is, are you willing?

☐ **IS THIS YOU?** (*Tick this box if this is how you see weight loss*)

VERSUS

THE 'ORGANIZED' MINDSET

Sharvari and Rakesh are two doctors who are married to each other, to their clinic (which they own) and to their diets. They were dedicated to the programme, lost the weight and have become a shining example to all those clients who tell me they cannot make space for weight loss in their life.

They were so happy with their increased energy levels (as well as with reaching their weight loss goals) that they took the lessons to heart. And back to the clinic. They realized that if you eat smaller meals frequently, you are at your maximum potential, as your energy levels are maintained and sugars are stable. With that in mind, they have made it compulsory for all doctors who are in surgery for more than two hours to be fed a biscuit during the surgery. The intern gets sterilized, the biscuit is sterilized, he goes to the OT, and they feed the doctor in the OT. It's one of the best examples I give my other busy clients. If a surgeon can do it during surgery, so can you.

One of the best parts about living in India is that we have excellent infrastructure for weight loss. Think about it. We have all the help we need. We have cooks and bais who we can delegate cooking to. There are dabba services if we don't live at home. And family support systems who can take over some of our responsibilities when we want to take an hour out for exercise. In fact, we have no excuse not to lose weight.

So what's left is the planning. In other words, you need to put a little thought into what you are going to eat in the day and when you need to exercise. Why walk to the corner for sev-puri when you have a veggies-and-dip snack in your bag? When you're organized, you have no excuses.

6. THE 'GRASS IS GREENER' MINDSET

You hate the feeling. The whole world's ordering fries and cheese-filled burgers, and here you are sitting through dinner sipping green tea, eating steamed rice and grilled fish. Argghhhhh! You stick to your game plan, resolute and stubborn. But the same two words play in your mind over and over again: Why me? Why me? Why me?

The 'Grass Is Greener' Mindset[6] is a bottomless pit of complete and total envy, where you are wildly jealous of other people's abilities to effortlessly maintain their weight while you have to work so hard at it. You become demoralized with the sacrifices you have been making, because you don't think anyone has it as tough as you do. You eventually get off the programme because you want to enjoy life like everyone else.

In a perfect world, it would be awesome if everyone who had a weight problem hung out, partied and lost weight together. But as you already know, weight loss can be an isolating experience. You're almost always surrounded by thinner people, or people for whom weight loss is not a priority. Or you are faced with millions of temptations, be it a TV commercial or mithai being offered by a well-meaning aunty. You are also unable to come to terms with the fact that you have to eat healthy for the rest of your life if you want to maintain the weight you have lost. That's when the prospect of healthy living depresses you. Life's too short, right?

☐ **IS THIS YOU?** (*Tick this box if this is how you see weight loss*)

VERSUS

THE 'MY GRASS IS GREENEST' MINDSET

After having counselled nearly 15,000 clients, I'm extremely happy to tell you that after a certain point in life, *everyone* has to take care of his or her health. If your childhood buddy has been inhaling French fries forever and still manages to stay in shape, it *will* catch up with

---

[6] Judith Beck, *The Beck DIET Solution*, Oxmoor House, 2008

him or her post 30 or 40. Because as we get older, our metabolism slows down. Our body changes. It's just a matter of time.

Besides, those who work at maintaining their bodies don't always tell you they are doing so. Sometimes they don't want to admit it. And sometimes, weight maintenance comes so naturally to them, they aren't even aware they are doing things to keep their weight down.

When you are laying the foundation for eating healthy earlier than others, you are giving yourself a chance to prevent disease earlier. You are setting healthy habits earlier. You have maintained a healthy weight for longer. Your friends or relatives will have to catch up with your way of living. You're just getting a head start.

And like I said before, when you've eaten healthy for long enough, and lost the weight you always wanted to, you will discover that life is about more than just food. When you're more active, getting more efficient, doing better at work, being more energetic, wearing fabulous clothes and doing things your body never allowed you to do before, you realize that the grass was greener on your side all along.

7. THE 'NO' MINDSET

OMG! A diet! More don'ts than dos!

The moment we start to make lifestyle changes, we panic. The 'No' Mindset refers to the belief that there are certain foods that will be banned for life. Because the association with dieting is about sacrifice and deprivation, you feel you will never get to eat your favourite foods again. *OMG*, you think, *I have to live the rest of my life without ice-cream, chocolate, pakodas, mithai?!!!! AAARRRRGHHHHH!!!!!* It's a depressing, demotivating thought and it is remarkably successful at getting you off your weight loss plan for good. If you look at weight loss as an endless foray into low-cal food, why should you be motivated to stick to your plan?

☐   **IS THIS YOU?** *(Tick this box if this is how you see weight loss)*

VERSUS

THE 'IT'S ALLOWED' MINDSET

When you fast, or when you give up something for a short period (such as for religious reasons), you know you can do it because you can see that at some definite point in the future, it will end. You reassure yourself and tell your body that this venture into abstinence has a definite end and that's what keeps you going.

You don't have to kill the cheesecakes, the high-calorie cocktails, the pakodas and samosas and throw them entirely out of your life. Remember that the body can be like a rebellious teenage brat. We don't like being told what we shouldn't have, and what we shouldn't do. It makes us want to go out and do it all the more. Why do you think overly stringent diets always fail? Because what you are doing is telling your body to say no to everything. You cannot expect your body to adjust to a situation where almost every food is suddenly forbidden. You're not being fair, either to yourself or to your body. And you are just left with higher, more insatiable cravings. It's a lose-lose situation.

Don't be stupid, be smart. Outsmart your body's instincts. When you have reached your goal weight, allow *everything* in moderation. You will never feel deprived if you are sending your brain the signal that everything's okay. The only thing you are doing is protecting your body from food it can tolerate regularly and keeping an eye on what it needs its space from.

WHAT'S YOUR SCORE?

How many 'mindsets' have you ticked? Even if you've ticked just one, this could be what was standing in your way all along.
Think about it.

What's Your Weight
Loss Dream?

Everyone who wants to lose weight has pictured themselves thinner a million times. Now it's your turn. This space is dedicated to crafting your weight loss dream, where you picture yourself at your dream weight. What will you be wearing, who will you be meeting, where will you be going, what will you be doing?

Visualization is an extremely effective technique to get you to your goal weight, and is used by people all over the world. When you visualize or 'see' yourself in your hot new body, you automatically replace negative thoughts – I'll never lose weight, I'm so fat – with positive ones – I'm in control of my eating, I'm in control of my weight, I call the shots – and you work towards your goal because you can *see* it.

Remember the visualization exercise from the previous chapter?

Visualize yourself at your goal weight. You're wearing that one dress or bikini or your wedding lehenga or that sharp double-breasted suit you have always wanted to wear. Imagine yourself stepping into a wedding or party. Picture how people will look at you, think of the compliments you will receive. Imagine how much lighter you will be feeling, how much faster you will be walking about. Focus on the reactions of those who have always made fun of your weight. And how their jaws drop as they see the new you.

Now use this example to develop your own weight loss dream. Imagine you've rolled out of bed one day, caught a glimpse of yourself in the mirror and... Wow! You realize you have reached your goal weight.

And Now That You Are Finally at Your Dream Weight...

What will you wear?

_____
_____
_____
_____

Where are you off to? To a party or a wedding or a beach vacation?

_____
_____
_____
_____

Who will you meet?

_____
_____
_____
_____

What will you do?

_____
_____
_____
_____

Who will check you out?

_____

_____

_____

_____

How will your friends and family react? Who do you think will be shocked or go green with envy? Who makes fun of you?

_____

_____

_____

_____

How will you feel once you've proved to the world that you did it? Who will be proud of you? Who will admire you?

_____

_____

_____

_____

How will you feel now that you are running or jumping or dancing or doing everything you have always wanted to do?

_____

_____

_____

_____

Don't hold back. There is nothing that is outside the realm of your imagination. Come back to this page *daily* and read what you have written to keep yourself focused. Your mind will get there. All your body has to do now is catch up.

FITTING INTO YOUR GENES

You are not always what you eat. Some of my clients put on weight due to genetic or medical reasons. Weight gain could be a symptom of a pre-existing medical condition like a metabolic disorder or a genetic predisposition or it could be indicative of a hormonal condition like Polycystic Ovarian Syndrome or PCOS. To tell these clients that they are gaining weight solely because of their eating habits is not a fair assessment.

What is unfair (to them) is that when some of them come in clutching their medical reports, they have already given up on their body. They have lost the battle in their head and come to me as a last resort or because their doctor has recommended nutritional changes. They come hoping to lose a few kilos here and there, hoping to cut down on their medication. They are understandably distressed and have little expectation of ever reaching their dream target.

What do I do in these situations? Do I treat them as special cases and whip up a whole new set of meal plans that my regular clients don't get? Do I ask my clients to locate difficult-to-find healthy ingredients from that one foreign store in that one by-lane of that one part of town? Do I expect less weight loss from these clients than I do from others?

The short answer is that I do nothing.

Nothing. Squat. Zero. Nada. Ille.

I treat them as I do any other client. They reach their dream targets anyway.

I'm not saying for one moment that I ignore their medical condition. Yes, there are certain foods that are contraindicated and every case is different. If, for example, their reports indicate high cholesterol or insulin resistance brought on by their condition, then appropriate steps need to be taken. When I say I treat them as any other client, I mean that I have the same expectations of weight loss from them (over the entire duration of their programme, although not necessarily on a month-to-month basis). I don't see why a client with PCOS should give me any less overall weight loss than someone without the condition. Or why I should go easy on someone with hypothyroidism.

In fact, there have been some cases where the speed at which my medical clients lose weight not only matches but, in some cases, outpaces my other clients. In front of me, I see them get the body they always wanted. They have been vigilant, set long-term healthy habits in place and been rewarded with beautifully maintained weight. And they have significantly cut down on their medication, too.

I know it's not always easy. And yes, it *can* take more time. They have to work a little harder than most. They have to make a few adjustments. But they don't have to stray very far from what everybody else eats. And they have successfully met their targets and then some. When you are medically or genetically prone towards obesity, weight gain may not always be in your hands. But weight loss is.

TRUST

It's Time to Trust Your Body

The best relationships are the ones founded on trust. Whether it's the ones we have with our friends, colleagues, parents or spouse or the one we have with our body, it's not a successful relationship if it is missing this key ingredient.

My clients often look suspiciously at me when I prescribe a meal plan that doesn't conform to stereotypical notions of what a diet should consist of. People with diabetes vigorously shake their heads when I begin to prescribe potatoes and rice. Teenage girls squeal when I tell them they need to eat eight times a day. We pass on the bread and skip carbs at night. We make a mountain out of a mango and a drama out of dessert. We fear food – so many foods – because we're not sure exactly what our body is going to do with it. So we stringently monitor what we eat, controlling what we do *from the outside* because we do not trust how our body works *from the inside.*

This section is called 'Trust' because trust is the first step to any successful weight loss programme. I've put this chapter before the chapter on nutrition because before I advise you on what to eat, I want you to trust your body with food. I want you to understand exactly what your body does with the food it eats, how it burns food, and how much of it gets burned without you lifting a finger. Not only can you eat more than you thought you could, you can eat things you never thought you could, all because your body needs them.

It's time to trust your body. It's time to understand that food is the only fuel for your beautiful body. You need to remember that your body works for YOU. It will lose the weight for you. All you have to do is set the right things in motion, and leave the rest to your body. If you gain trust, you will lose weight. Trust me.

Trusting Your Body | Lesson 1

Your body is beautiful, complex and is always working. For you.

A phone call is not just a phone call if you observe how your body reacts to dialling a number. When you use your index finger to dial, you activate not one but *seven* muscles that control its movement. Hundreds of thousands of electrical signals are set in motion as nerve cells in your spinal cord command your finger to move from number to number. And all this furious activity takes place in less than a fraction of a second.

When you laugh, you immediately pump 'feel-good hormones' – endorphins – into your blood as your body is enveloped by a heightened sense of well-being. Fifteen facial muscles contract when you smile even as you're boosting your immune system.

The body is a beautiful, living, breathing machine. There is symphony, harmony, marriage and melody, and in its inherent complexity is the simple fact that with everything we do, our body is working 24x7 to perform its numerous brilliant functions. With the stress of everyday living, we forget the wonder and magic that form the human body.

Food accidently goes down the windpipe? Our body's instinctive reflex is to cough it out. Dust in our eye? Our tear ducts go into overdrive to protect our eyes. Our body generates millions of antibodies to guard us from disease and death. It comes with its own inbuilt mechanisms to protect us as much as it can.

What has this got to do with weight loss? Well, when we start our weight loss programme and don't immediately lose the amount we wanted to, it's easy to lose faith in our body. The same programme works differently on different bodies and we have to believe that our body is acting as fast as it can and that weight loss is on its way. This is the first part of trusting our body – remembering that it is always working for us. And that we can be who we are – and as thin as we want to be – because our body makes everything possible.

Chew on this

Tick the options you think are correct. You can find the answers at the bottom of the next page.

1. Your skin helps regulate the temperature of your body by making your pores bigger when it's hot and smaller when it's cold.
    ☐ True   ☐ False

2. Your immune system protects you from millions of
    ☐ Bacteria
    ☐ Viruses
    ☐ Toxins
    ☐ Parasites
    ☐ All of the above

3. The hair in your nostrils is designed to
    ☐ Filter the air you breathe in
    ☐ Protect you from airborne bacteria
    ☐ Both of the above
    ☐ It has no function

4. Your tonsils protect you from infection by trapping germs coming in through your nose and mouth.
    ☐ True   ☐ False

5.   **You need fat. Essential fats**
    ☐ Protect your brain, liver and heart
    ☐ Regulate your body temperature
    ☐ Lubricate your joints
    ☐ All of the above

Trusting Your Body | Lesson 2

Food gives you life. How can you be afraid of what gives you life?

One of the simplest functions in your body is metabolism, i.e., your body burns what you eat. Whether you are making a phone call, standing in line at the multiplex or shopping for vegetables, you are burning, burning, burning. You breathe, you burn. You smile, you burn. You stick your tongue out at a kid making faces at you, you burn. Even when you're complaining about your body, whether you're talking about it or crying about it, you burn. If you're living and breathing, rest assured that you are burning calories every second of every day.

To me, this is *the* fundamental lesson: food is not calories, weight gain or fat. Food and water are the only source of nourishment for millions of cells that work non-stop, second by second, hour by hour. Food is nutrition, fuel, nourishment, and it is there for your inherent good. Food is about what it does *for* your body, and not just what it does *to* it. The moment you understand this is the moment you start to heal your relationship with food.

Using the example in the previous lesson, when we dial that number and make that phone call, we also set a chain reaction of electrical impulses in motion. Vitamins and minerals are crucial components to making these linkages happen. So, if your 'processing' time becomes slower, or your 'reactions' slow down, it could well be because of a vitamin or mineral deficiency. Many health problems, whether minor (acidity, gas, giddiness, fatigue, nausea) or major (diabetes, cardiovascular, hypertension, cancer) are lifestyle-related and depend on what you eat or don't eat. Compromised eating is compromised functioning for your body. And compromised functioning will impact every aspect of your life.

What all this means is that you should never be afraid of food. So many foods have their own properties and benefits and when people cut carbs or go non-fat, they have already decided that certain foods are their 'enemy'. It disturbs me when clients make weight loss a battle with food when it should be just a battle with the bulge.

Chew on this

1. Your body works 24x7. And if it's working, it's burning.
2. Even while you sleep, you burn calories. There's even a metabolic calculation for it, and it's called RMR or Resting Metabolic Rate.
3. Can you imagine how much you would burn just by increasing your activity levels?
4. You are literally what you eat. Your moods, your energy, your stamina, your reactions to every activity depend on how and what you've eaten in the last 45 to 110 minutes.
5. Vitamins and minerals are essential for making the connections between your brain and the rest of your body. Deficiency in potassium – a condition called hypokalemia – has been attributed to the slowing down of reactions and response times.

Trusting Your Body | Lesson 3

Eat and delete: 'free' calorie burn

Each and every body is blessed with its own 'free' calorie burn which is called BMR or Basal Metabolic Rate. Your BMR is the minimum amount of food your body needs to perform its necessary chemical reactions and its life-giving metabolic functions (that's why it's called 'Basal'). I call BMR 'Eat and Delete' because it is the minimum amount of food the body will burn at rest, irrespective of physical activity. This is 'free' calorie burn; if you eat, so shall your body 'delete'.

Take my client Tejas, for example. At 5 feet 11 inches, this 27-year-old IT engineer is of medium build and weighs 70 kilos. If he wants to do nothing on Sunday but lie in bed, he still burns 1740 calories just by virtue of being a living, breathing human being. So, just lying in bed and doing nothing else burns over 1700 calories for a 70-kilo man. All he has to do is eat about 1740 calories and it will have *zero* impact on his weight.

Eat = Delete.

So What's Your 'Eat and Delete' Number?

Before starting any weight loss programme, the first thing I (or any nutritionist) will do is calculate your BMR because that gives you a starting point for losing weight. The higher your BMR, the more your body burns at rest. And the more your body burns at rest, the more of what you eat gets burned in a day. Find out your BMR by using the following equation (This is the only bit of math I am going to make you do in this book, I swear!):

Calculate Your BMR

HARRIS-BENEDICT EQUATION

Women's BMR	Men's BMR
655	66
+ (9.6 × your weight in kilos)	**+** (13.7 × your weight in kilos)
+ (1.8 × your height in cm)	**+** (5 × your height in cm)
− (4.7 × your age in years)	**−** (6.8 × your age in years)
= _____calories per day	**=** _____calories per day

KATCH-MCARDLE FORMULA FOR BMR

If you're very overweight or very muscular, the standard Harris-Benedict equation might not work for you. The Katch-McArdle formula for estimation of BMR is far more accurate in these cases. To arrive at your BMR, first subtract your body fat in kilos from your current weight in kilos. You will then get your lean muscle mass. Second, calculate your BMR using the following formula.

BMR = 370 + (21.6 × lean mass in kilos)

This formula applies to both men and women.

Trusting Your Body | Lesson 4

If you think you're stuck with your BMR, you're not.

By just looking at the previous lesson, it is clear that your 'Eat and Delete' number is determined by:

❏ *How tall you are.* The taller you are, the higher your BMR.
❏ *How old you are.* If you're wondering why you are gaining weight despite following the same eating patterns, it probably has to do with your age. Unfortunately, the older

we get, the lower our BMR becomes. After the age of 20, it drops about 2 per cent every decade.

❏ *Whether you're male or female.* Sorry ladies, but this is a fact. Men have higher BMRs than women, because their bodies have a higher percentage of muscle.

❏ *How much you weigh.* The heavier you are, the higher your BMR. But this is a bit misleading so I need to explain. The additional weight taxes your body and it needs more calories to perform its basic functions. If you weigh 20 kilos more than you are supposed to, you need to sustain the extra weight with extra calories.

I can almost hear you say: 'Are you telling me that what determines my BMR is set in stone? Age, height, gender – how can I change those?!' Well, not exactly. While it is true that your BMR is more or less dependent on factors you cannot change, there are still two things you can do to change your metabolic rate:

1. Build Muscle

'I swear I don't eat more than my friends. Yet I'm the only one who can't fit into a bikini. Why does everything happen to ME!'

No, the universe is not conspiring against you. If we rule out genetic and other factors contributing to your weight gain, it all boils down to how much body fat you have as opposed to your friends. If I have two female clients, both 20 years old, both 160 cm tall and at the same weight, both their BMRs would come to 1300 calories. But if the body composition of the first girl is 30 per cent fat and that of the second is 20 per cent, it means the second girl has more muscle. And if she has more muscle, she is going to burn more than 1300 calories.

Muscle is more 'expensive' to maintain. Your body has to work harder and therefore uses more calories – or needs more food –

to maintain more muscle. To maintain the fat in your body, your body uses 'x' calories. But to maintain muscle, your body uses '3x' the number of calories. That means, when you are at rest, or doing nothing at all, your body burns *three* times the number of calories for every pound of muscle. Is that a good deal, or what? Conversely, your metab decreases by about 0.01 calories/ minute for every per cent increase in body fat. So the more fat you have, the lower your BMR gets.

If you want to boost your BMR, you need to cut fat as well as build muscle. But if you think you'll be bench-pressing weights the size of a small building, beefing up at the gym, scarfing down raw egg yolk and imbibing other crazy routines, calm down and take a deep breath – you don't have to do any of that. Light-weight training two or three times a week is all you need to get your BMR going.

By working on your muscles, you are 'delegating' weight loss to your body – your body will burn more calories than it does at the moment, even as you do nothing but lie around all day, making you the boss of your weight loss.

2. Eat Smart

Here, the only heavy-lifting you get to do is when you 'lift' food into your mouth. Did you know that just by changing your pattern of eating, you can lose weight? That, by eating frequently, eating smart and eating certain foods, you can enhance – and alter – your BMR? In the following pages, I have highlighted these as separate lessons so you get a better idea of how to make what you eat work for you.

Chew on this

How much body fat do you have?

Go online to calculate your body fat percentage. Any good health website will have a good body fat calculator.

This table should give you a general idea about where you stack up:

WOMEN

Age	Underfat	Healthy Range	Overweight	Obese
20–40 yrs	Under 21%	21-33%	33-39%	Over 39%
41–60 yrs	Under 23%	23-35%	35-40%	Over 40%
61–79 yrs	Under 24%	24-36%	36-42%	Over 42%

MEN

Age	Underfat	Healthy Range	Overweight	Obese
20–40 yrs	Under 8%	8-19%	19-25%	Over 25%
41–60 yrs	Under 11%	11-22%	22-27%	Over 27%
61–79 yrs	Under 13%	13-25%	25-30%	Over 30%

Source: http://lowcarbdiets.about.com/library/blbodyfatcharts.htm, accessed on 12/1/12

However, do note that while online body fat calculators are good estimates, they are never fully accurate. For an accurate body fat analysis, get a DEXA test done at a clinic. Alternatively, most gyms are equipped with machines that analyse your body fat, which are good but, again, not as accurate as a clinical DEXA test.

A BIG FAT STORY

Fat is unfortunately the *only* way our bodies have evolved to store unutilized calories or energy. It converts whatever it cannot use, be it sugar, carbohydrates or dietary fat itself, into body fat and starts to tuck it away in places on your body that are the most okay with hosting it. Where your body is more prone to storing fat is the difference between what makes you an apple – with abdominal fat, which is more common among men – and a pear – with fat on your hips and thighs, which makes more women than men tear their hair out. For every 3500 calories that have not been utilized by your body and are therefore stored, you gain a pound of fat. And it creeps up on you because your body stores fat little by little.

But why *does* the body store fat the way it does? Why can't it just burn more fat or expel the fat out of the system?

How and why we store fat has a lot to do with human evolution and the problem of scarcity of food. Historically, the human race was faced with conditions that we simply don't have to deal with in today's culture of excess. But dial back to hundreds of years ago, when there were long periods of drought and famine, and the problem was not about eating too much but about getting enough to eat in the first place. As a result, the human body pushed the panic button and started storing unused calories as fat so that, in the advent of further deprivation, it could fuel the body from these 'reserves'.

Think of your body as a good host, and excess fat as a bad guest. Your body is very accommodating and will keep hosting more and more fat 'guests'. And fat doesn't get the hint. You have to kick it out of your house. Or you will always have extra mouths (i.e., fat cells) to feed.

Right now, for most of us, whether it's food or consumption or information overload, there is simply too much of too much. Portion sizes are getting bigger as corporations want to be seen as providing Value for Money; food has become entertainment; there are just too many brands, sizes and value packs competing for your attention; and lifestyles have become more sedentary. Even as our immediate environment has evolved, our bodies have not caught up. As path-breaking health specialist Dr Dean Ornish said, 'Weighing too much is a relatively modern problem.'*

---

* Dean Ornish, *Eat More, Weigh Less*, Quill, 2001

THE SKINNY ON FAT

Not all fat is created alike. And knowing the difference could be the difference between life and death.

Subcutaneous Fat is the fat you see, and it parks itself right under your skin (hence 'subcutaneous'). It is the most visible aspect of weight gain and it is the fat that alters your body shape. 'Love handles', 'saddle bags', 'tyres' and so on are manifestations of subcutaneous fat.

Visceral Fat is a silent predator, the fat you can't see, but it is far more lethal. It lines your organs, like the liver, kidneys or pancreas. Extensive research has shown that people whose bodies contain a higher percentage of visceral fat are more likely to develop diabetes, cancer, high BP and cardio-vascular complications. When visceral fat breaks down, the rate at which it oxidises, i.e., the rate at which oxygen is removed from hydrogen as fat gets broken down in the body, results in the production of free radicals. These free radicals – which are single-cell oxygen atoms – are dangerous. They are like wild animals on the rampage, attacking any organs they like, causing destruction in their wake.

If you're an apple (big waist, thin legs), chances are you might have more visceral fat. The torso is where all your organs are and if this is where your fat settles down, you need to get moving on losing weight and eating healthy. Bottom line: if you look like an apple, it's time to start eating one.

Trusting Your Body | Lesson 5

If you starve, you won't burn

This lesson is crucial for all you crash-dieters. While muscle builds your BMR, starving yourself has the exact opposite effect: it lowers your BMR. Which is why crash-dieting works only as long as you are, well, crash-dieting. Drastic calorie cuts will never allow you to succeed in managing long-term weight loss. In fact, the only thing you will succeed in doing is making things worse.

If you take your average soup-and-salad diet, it will account for approximately 800 calories per day, which is starving your body. You must remember that when I say 'starvation,' I'm not just talking about complete and absolute deprivation of food. Starvation can also be relative. Your body can starve even when you think you're getting enough. If your body BMR is 1400 but you're eating at 800, you have suddenly deprived your body of 600 calories that it needs, and have now gone into starvation mode, or what I call the Generator Mode.

Generator Mode

If your house is suddenly plunged into darkness, you need a generator to get things going. And if you are using a generator, you can't switch on all the appliances in your house at once. You can switch on the fan, but you can't switch on the AC. You'll prioritize and use what you need the most, right? With 800 calories, your body can't sustain its normal circulation or perform its usual functions like breathing, circulation, digestion and so on. You automatically start using less energy for the same purposes. For example, if you ideally use 60 per cent of your energy output for breathing, you will now use less. Or if you use 40 per cent for circulation, you will use less. So when you drastically cut calories, your body moves from full burning to compromised burning, or a slower metabolic rate. Your body can't burn fat because fat burning by itself is a high metabolic rate process. So if your body can't use fat, it will use the next best thing: muscle.

Why Losing Muscle Is Such a Big Deal

It's a chain reaction. When you starve to lose weight, you lose muscle mass. When you lose muscle mass, you are decreasing an efficient calorie-burning part of your body. The more muscle you lose, the more your fat cells increase, i.e., the lost muscle is replaced by fat. The more your fat cells increase, the less efficient your body becomes at burning calories at rest. And the more fat cells you have, the greater your body's tendency to store even *more* fat the moment you get 'off' your diet. Yikes!

Understanding the Role of Starvation in Weight Gain

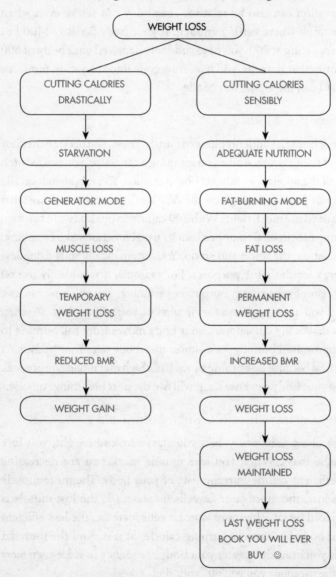

That's why you yo-yo. That's why you gain even more weight later when you lose weight incorrectly. That's why *fat loss* is as important as *weight loss*. And that's why losing even a gram of muscle is not what we want to do. Because if you want it gone forever, it has to be fat. If you want to lose weight by losing muscle, be prepared for it to come back. And then some.

Chew on this

1. **If you lose weight by starving, your body will eventually**
   a. Lose muscle, gain fat
   b. Lose fat, gain muscle
   c. Lose weight, lose fat
   d. All of the above

2. **Food for thought:**
   What's more important: fat loss or weight loss?

Trusting Your Body | Lesson 6

Digestion burns calories

If breathing, sleeping and smiling burn calories, can digestion be far behind?

Forget running on the treadmill, digestion is a calorie-burning activity on its own. Consider this: for every calorie you ingest, your body uses some of the same calories you eat to burn what you are eating. It's like shopping and getting a partial refund the second you swipe your card! The question is, how do you make this wonderful feature of your body work for you; and how do you increase the refund?

This is the essential principle behind the practice of frequent eating where eating at shorter intervals enables your body to use

Answer: 1.a

GIVE BIRTH TO BABIES, NOT PROBLEMS

When women starve themselves, or eat way below their BMR, their bodies don't just lose muscle. One of the first effects of malnourishment is the toll it takes on a woman's reproductive system. The moment she starts to lose sight of her nourishment, her body hits back with irregular menstrual cycles. But why does this happen?

During ovulation, a woman's body prepares the uterus to conceive a baby by lining the wall of the uterus with tissues. When she doesn't conceive, these tissues break down and she bleeds every month. But with starvation or malnourishment, the body cannot create this lining properly. When the lining is not thick enough, the periods become irregular or scant and the reproductive system starts shutting down.

And that's just the tip of the iceberg. Crash-dieting has been associated with problems in conception, increasing the possibilities of miscarriage and premature birth. Side effects of eating disorders like bulimia are so severe they prevent women from having healthy children in future.

Food doesn't just sustain the body. It sustains the body's ability to produce life. If a woman doesn't eat enough to sustain her own body, how will she take care of another body? That's why fad diets almost always impact the reproductive system. If women want to give birth to babies and not problems, there should be no ill-advised starvation or deprivation. Period.

more calories to aid digestion. When you constantly give your body fuel, it means you are constantly tickling your body to work. Keep working, keep working, keep burning, keep burning. This is called the thermogenic effect of food and it is not only an incredibly smart way of losing weight, it also helps you increase your BMR.

I like to call this the Internal Workout – because by constantly making it work to digest food, you're giving your body a workout. And while you may not be able to see the furious digestive activity going on in your body at any point in time, trust me, your body is working way harder than if you eat at longer intervals.

There are two ways to make your digestive system burn even more calories:

How Much We Eat

Let's not consider *what* we're eating for now. Whether the food is high in trans fats or sugars, we gain weight because our body can only metabolize a certain amount of food at a time – a maximum of 300 to 500 calories per meal.* So, for example, if you eat a lunch of two chapatis, dal, dahi and sabzi, your body needs to be fuelled by that and only that. Forget chocolate or cheesecake, even if you decide to finish your meal with fruit, it will get stored as fat because your body has been fuelled to its optimum until this point. It doesn't need any more food. Anything additional gets stored as fat. Which is why portion control is so necessary.

I've had so many clients who take my meal plan and 'save' up their calories for a heavy dinner or brunch and compensate by only having soup at night. But that doesn't work. What you're essentially doing to your body by eating too much at one go is storing the excess as fat, and if you're compensating by eating soup at night, your body goes into starvation mode and you start losing muscle. In other words, your 'balance sheet' is not accrued at the end of every day, but at the end of every meal.

What We Eat

Challenge your digestion. Whether it's rice, ice-cream, French fries or Coke, *every single thing* you ingest is absorbed and burned at a different rate of metabolism by your body, so you can bump up your BMR simply by choosing the right foods. The harder it is to **challenge** your **digestion** digest, the more calories your body burns in trying to digest it. And that's the key – to eat those foods that make your body *work* to digest them.

* Depending on your BMR

Foods high in fibre challenge your digestive system by raising your metabolic rate by almost 10 per cent. If you eat food that contains a greater amount of carbohydrates or fats, your metabolic rate increases by about 4 per cent. And here's the kicker – proteins elevate metabolic rates by up to 30 per cent because the process of breaking them down is more 'labour intensive'. And what's more, all these calories are expended from your fat reserves.

Conversely, simple carbohydrates like sugary foods don't put up much of a fight. These foods get absorbed into your system so fast, your body doesn't have to work to digest them. The same goes for food that is high in fat. The fat you eat gets stored as fat because 'fat is how you store energy'.[7] Putting it another way, let's say two people eat food that contain the same number of calories. If the food of the first person has higher fat content, his or her body will store *more* fat than the second person. It's that simple.

However, fruits and vegetables are complex sugars. To digest them, your body has to first break poly- and di-sugars down to mono-sugars, which requires energy, and subsequently more calories are burned by your body.

But don't go all out and have meat-only or high-protein diets or completely banish fat from your menu. The worldwide consensus on the dangers of high protein diets like Atkins have been well-documented and make convincing arguments as to why you need to chill out on your protein intake. Any meal plan that has an unfair skew towards *any* food group, including protein or raw veggies, will give rise to a host of medical problems and will have a diminishing effect on your system. If you think it's unbalanced, it is. And you cannot be shortsighted about this fact because it *will* catch up with you.

---

[7] Dean Ornish, *Eat More, Weigh Less*, Quill, 2001

Chew on this

1. Listed below are foods with similar calorie counts. What food choices would YOU make for a better calorie burn?

   1. ☐ Apple   or   ☐ A slice of toast

   2. ☐ Grapefruit   or   ☐ 2 to 3 biscuits

   3. ☐ Orange juice   or   ☐ Egg white

   4. ☐ Khakra   or   ☐ Sugar candy

   5. ☐ Sabudana   or   ☐ Bowl of bran flakes

Trusting Your Body | Lesson 7

Eating every two hours ups your BMR

I find that over 90 per cent of my clients show me the best results when they split their food plan over ten small meals a day. So whether it's punctuating your main meals with fruit or a few biscuits, these two-hour windows provide just the right intervals not only for weight loss, but also for maintaining your blood sugar. If you don't see a change in your weight for years even though you have been eating the same foods, break up your 3 to 4 meals into 8 to 10 meals. You'll be surprised at the results.

Eating every two hours ensures that your blood sugar levels never dip, and also wards off the onset of too much insulin production. If you do a check of any person on any one of my diets, their sugar levels will be stable through the day. There will never be peaks and troughs. That's because the body is constantly and consistently fuelled. And if it's consistently fuelled and you feel full, you won't cheat.

Three-hour intervals are not frequent enough, because to eat every three hours, you need to have larger meals. As we know,

Answers: 1. Apple 2. Grapefruit 3. Egg white 4. Khakra 5. Bowl of bran flakes the body can digest only a certain amount of food at a time and the rest gets stored as fat. If you are going to eat larger meals, that particular digestion cycle is going to lead to more fat storage, which is not what you want.

In fact, for some of my clients, hourly diets work. I even get them to break their lunch. So they'll have dal-chawal at 1 p.m., followed by roti-sabzi at 2 p.m., and only then do their bodies respond. But two-hour intervals work for most people, and very few people need hourly diets.

The converse is not true. I had a client who wanted to carry a glass of chhaas and some channa and eat that through the day, sometimes even at intervals of 20 minutes. That doesn't work. Because then your body isn't getting enough time to digest in the first place so the fat burning can't take place. There need to be appropriate intervals between eating for the body to start burning fat. And two is my magic number.

Chew on this

1. List all the food you eat in the day at the time you eat it.
   BREAKFAST (___a.m.) _____
   LUNCH (___p.m.) _____
   TEATIME (___p.m.) _____
   DINNER (___p.m.) _____

2. To kickstart your weight loss and to start seeing results, split the same foods listed above into smaller meals.
   7 a.m. _____
   9 a.m. _____
   11 a.m. _____
   1 p.m. _____
   3 p.m. _____
   5 p.m. _____
   7 p.m. _____
   9 p.m. _____

WAHEEDA REHMAN ON
EATING EVERY TWO HOURS

I think eating every two hours has changed my life. It has given me a lot of energy. You don't tend to overeat because you are eating something or the other every two hours. You feel healthy and you lose weight.

Trusting Your Body | Lesson 8

Leptin, ghrelin, insulin: your weight management hormones

Leptin. Ghrelin. Insulin. Three biggies in the hormone department which can wreak havoc with your diet or help you maintain it beautifully.

Leptin is the hormone that gives you the signal that your body is full. Ghrelin is the hormone that tells you your body needs food. Leptin and ghrelin work hand in hand to regulate your hunger and satiety levels. When you have low levels of leptin, you never feel full. When you have high levels of ghrelin, your body mistakenly thinks it needs to eat more, especially sugary foods. If you feel like you are eating more than usual or you keep reaching for those cakes and biscuits, get yourself checked – it could be symptomatic of low leptin or high ghrelin.

Insulin is produced by the pancreas and its job is that of a messenger, taking nutrients from the bloodstream and transporting them to the body's cells for storage. However, if you have too much insulin, it puts a halt on your body's fat-burning process. When you eat too much sugary stuff like cakes or sweets, your blood sugar spikes. Insulin production increases in crazy amounts, because it tries to remove the glucose from your bloodstream and send it to your body's cells for storage, like it stores everything else. But after it has removed the glucose, your sugar levels plunge, leaving you feeling like you want more sugar. It's a vicious cycle and it could lead to insulin resistance, obesity and Type II diabetes.

If you look at the above, it's clear that what you eat plays a huge role in keeping these hormones on their best behaviour. Slow down on the sugary foods. Just making this small change could get your hunger, satiety and blood sugar levels under control, leading you to manage your diet better and keeping you on the path of healthy eating.

Chew on this

Did you know that the best way to treat low leptin and high ghrelin levels is to get a good night's sleep, eat small meals, reduce your stress and maintain a good random blood sugar level?

Trusting Your Body | Lesson 9

Eating after exercise burns more calories

This is one of the simplest tricks in the book. How much food the body can burn could also depend on when you eat it – before or after exercise. When you exercise, your body continues burning calories long after you've stepped off the treadmill. In fact, your BMR is enhanced for three hours after your workout session, which means more calories are burned by eating just after exercise. In other words, the same foods will metabolize faster. So not only have you worked out and lost weight, your body continues the burn. Two for the price of one!

Many think that by exercising *after* a meal, the calories will burn off. This is untrue. In fact, exercising to 'work off' what you have just eaten interferes with the process of digestion and doesn't burn as much as you would if you had waited to eat post your workout.

It is also not recommended to exercise on an empty stomach. When you wake up, your body has not been fuelled for 7 to 10 hours straight. If you push your body too hard without eating anything, the body goes into starvation mode and starts burning muscle when you exercise, and not just fat. You must eat something small on waking before exercise, whether it's half a fruit or a small portion of something healthy just to jumpstart your body. And then breakfast like a king after your workout because that's when your BMR is peaking.

Finally – and this is just a shout out to those who take naps after their workout – take advantage of your body after exercising. Your body is in calorie-burning mode and if you sleep after exercise your body burns far less than it would have if you were awake.

Reschedule your exercise

Jumpstart your calorie burn simply by rescheduling when you work out. Circle a new time to work out.

1.	BEFORE BREAKFAST			
	6 a.m.	7 a.m.	8 a.m.	10 a.m.

2.	BEFORE LUNCH			
	11 a.m.	12 noon	1 p.m.	2 p.m.

3.	BEFORE TEATIME			
	3 p.m.	4 p.m.	5 p.m.	

4.	BEFORE DINNER			
	7 p.m.	8 p.m.	9 p.m.	

Tip: Try adjusting your meal times to accommodate your new workout schedule.

Trusting Your Body | Lesson 10

Your body responds to exercise. Immediately.

It is an inescapable truth. No matter what or how carefully you eat, you can't ignore the simple fact that you need to Get Moving to Get Losing. The facts and figures that surround your body's response to exercise are mind-boggling. Did you know that:

❑ During any sort of brisk cardio activity like walking or jogging, your working muscles could use up to 25 times more energy than they would do at rest? In fact, a short burst of exercise like a 50- or 100-metre sprint needs 120 times more energy than usual! This is why interval training is so popular.

❑ During exercise, your heart beats faster, and pumps more blood into your muscles and other tissues. During intensive exercise, your heartbeat can rise up to 150 beats per minute (almost double the normal rate).

❑ The average heart pumps approximately 5 litres blood per minute. This amount may increase to almost 20 litres per minute during vigorous exercise.

❑ Depending on how hard you're working out, your metabolic rate goes up by about 4 to 20 times your resting metabolic rate. That's 20 times the calorie burn!

❑ Exercise is not the high-intensity investment of time it is made out to be. From taking the stairs instead of the lift to walking about while talking on the phone, you can lose weight simply by incorporating exercise into your lifestyle. Weight loss, like weight gain, is cumulative and even the smallest attempt to get out and get moving will show you benefits in the long run.

However, beware of a proportionate increase in calorie intake 'because I work out now'. Typically, people always underestimate how much they are eating, and overestimate how much they are burning.

Keeping the weight off is about finding joy in your physical activity, and realizing that if you do anything, *anything* that gets you moving, you have already burned more than you otherwise would. Find the exercise that works for you, so long as you can dedicate some amount of time to it on a weekly basis.

Chew on this

Guess how many calories are burned per hour for a person weighing 70 kilos. The results will surprise you!

1. **Sitting**

    ☐ 71 calories ☐ 82 calories ☐ 28 calories

2. **Standing**

    ☐ 97 calories ☐ 56 calories ☐ 12 calories

3. **Brisk walking (at 5 km/ hour)**

    ☐ 210 calories ☐ 280 calories ☐ 329 calories

4. **Light activity (such as office work or cooking)**

    ☐ 210 calories ☐ 246 calories ☐ 119 calories

5. **Cycling (at 10 km/ hour)**

    ☐ 188 calories ☐ 246 calories ☐ 217 calories

Answers: 1. 82 calories 2. 97 calories 3. 329 calories 4. 246 calories 5. 246 calories (Calories Burned Calculator, http://www.healthcalculators.org/calculators/calories_burned.asp, accessed on 12/2/12)

Later on in this book, I will help you choose food that will not just help you lose weight but also ensure that you don't feel deprived, so that you don't feel like you are making the sacrifice of a lifetime.

I believe that no matter how much you weigh, it's important to take a deep breath, smile and trust your body. Remember that simply by being alive you are burning, burning, burning.

INVEST

So When Do You Start?

Now.

Break Up with Your Food Past

When you've identified that you have an unhealthy relationship with food, it's time to set the stage for your food future. And the only way to do that is to break up with your food past. Until now, you have been treating food like a lover, an escape, an entertainer, a boss and entrusting it with your deepest, darkest secrets. Treat your relationship with unhealthy eating like one with a toxic boyfriend or girlfriend. And dump it like one.

'We Need to Talk'

It's a conversation no one likes to have. But if you really want to get rid of these habits and establish new ones, you have to evaluate what's going wrong. As in any situation, denial is not going to help you. You need to be brutally honest with the way your relationship with food is going. All you need to do is make a note. Write it down. It's that simple.

Take a book. Set aside seven pages and on each page map out what you eat every day for one week, Monday to Sunday. Everything. Whether it's a handful of peanuts, two chips, 4 tablespoons of boondi raita – every single thing. And note the time. This is an investment, trust me. Because it will make you conscious of how much you put into your mouth, even if you think you're watching what you eat. I've counselled many clients who say they are extremely calorie-conscious and only eat salad when they go out. A Caesar salad with all the trimmings can sometimes account for almost 900 calories – that's more than half your daily recommended calorie intake, not to mention that it overshoots your daily recommended fat allowance by 600 per cent! You're better off eating a burger without cheese.

Next, make a note of when you feel hungry the most. This info is going to be crucial when negotiating your weight loss goals. Your cravings peak and trough through different times of the day. Make a list of the times in the day when you feel the hungriest and start planning. My cravings spike from 5 to 7 p.m. and this is when I eat the most. Some of my clients are after-dinner snackers. Getting a fix on this 'craving time' is crucial because the success or failure of your new lifestyle depends on how you prepare for the moment when you have the weakest resistance to food. Hold onto this list because what you have is the beginning of a whole new relationship with food, a relationship we will re-examine in a bit.

When Are You at Your Hungriest?

8 a.m.

10 a.m.

12 p.m.

3 p.m

5 p.m

7 p.m

9 p.m

'It's Not You, It's Me'

Okay, show of hands. How many of you have used this as an excuse to break up with someone? This might be a time-honoured manoeuvre to dump someone gently, but when it comes to unhealthy eating patterns, it could not be closer to the truth. You can say what you like about genes and environment and time and hormones but at the end of the day, your relationship with food is all about you.

Write an open letter to food. Talk to it like it's a person. Use this space to pledge to change your relationship with it once and for all – don't end it, just *change* it.

Dear Food,

It's not you, it's me. While I love you, I want you to understand that you are not my escape or my boss. You are my friend: a very dear friend who is going to be a huge support in my weight loss journey by being there for me at the right time and in the right measure.

What You Are Not

(Use this space to define the negative and controlling role that food may have in your life currently)

1. My boss

2. Someone who controls me, what I do and when I do it

3. Someone I am emotionally dependent on

4.

5.

6.

What I Want You to Be

1.   A way to nourish my body
_____

2.   Someone I can call on when I need it
_____

3.   Someone who respects my time
_____

4.
_____

5.
_____

6.
_____

Your FRIEND,

_____(Your name)

We've started it off for you, but this is just an example. You can write it any which way you like.

'Let's Be Friends'

Your life is made up of all sorts of friends: the nerd, the shopaholic, the one you can call at 3 a.m., the one who has seen you through drunken binges and toxic relationships. You've got to use the same logic with food. Food exists in all kinds of shapes, sizes and forms. Some you need to be acquaintances with, some you can be good friends with, and some you can be best friends with. But the good news is you can be friends with all kinds of food. Just as you plan your social life, plan your food friends.

Best Friends
What you can eat on a daily basis

Rice Roti Bread Upma Kurmura Dalia
Cornflakes Popcorn Noodles Poha Bhel
Spaghetti Wholewheat pasta Vegetables Potato
Peas Chicken Fish Turkey Dal Moong Channa

Rajma **Grapes** Mangoes Bananas **Paneer**
Skimmed milk Curd **Egg white** Quinoa
Khus khus **Sweet Potato** Rava Sooji Bajra Jowar
Rahi **Biscuit** Momo

Good Friends
You can hang out with these once or twice a week
Cheese Dessert **Chocolate** **Muffin** Fried food
Pizza Prawns Cake Ice-cream **Samosa**
Batata vada **Pakoda** Fried wanton **Jalebi**

Acquaintances
You can air-kiss these foods once a month
Lard **Bacon** Beef Mutton **Pork** Shellfish
Smoothie **Fruit juice** Aerated beverages
ANYTHING ELSE YOU WANT!*

Now look at the list you made in 'We Need to Talk' and see where you're going wrong. Are you being overfamiliar with your acquaintances? Have you been ignoring your best friends? Or have you been giving your good friends a little too much importance? While the names of the friends are quite general, this is an excellent guide to where you are going wrong. When you are losing weight, rely on your good and best friends for support. Only they will be able to see you through. So we won't be air-kissing acquaintances during the weight loss phase. If you were facing a crisis, who would you rely on? Your good friends or your casual acquaintances? Think about it. And don't worry, I'll show you how to become closer to your acquaintances when you've lost the weight you planned on losing.

* This is just a rough list and is not exhaustive. The point of this is to give you a general idea of frequency of consumption.

The A to Z of A to B
Goal Setting

It doesn't matter who they are or what they do, almost everyone who visits my clinic for a consultation is armed with that one magic number.

'I have to come down to 56 kilos'
'I have to get into my size-24 jeans from college'
'Zero is my number. Size zero!'
'Five kilos a month. That's my target.'

What's remarkable about this approach is that everyone comes with *one* number. Not two or three or four. Very few people tell me they would like to come down to *approximately* 55 to 60 kilos or a size 6 *or* 8. There's no either/ or. There is just *one* goal. Anything else would mean failure.

Think about the pressure you are putting on yourself. In addition to work, family responsibilities and generally going about life, you are giving yourself so much 'weight loss' stress. Here you are, trying to fit into that Little Black Dress or killer suit for your college reunion with the hope of reversing *years* of weight gain in *weeks*. I mean, I have clients who come in at 81 kilos with a stringent target of losing 30 kilos in six months.

And they haven't even started.

And do you know what the worst part is? *You* set that goal. *You* gave yourself that kind of stress. *You* set yourself up for inevitable failure. Relax. Chill. Lose weight at a realistic, gradual pace; a pace you are comfortable with. Anti-quick fix your goals. The minute you set easier, more attainable targets, you will automatically feel the weight lift off your shoulders. And very soon, off your scale too.

A to A or A to B?

On the face of it, weight loss is nothing but a transition from Point A (your current weight) to Point B (your goal weight). But somewhere between A and B, many of us lose our way. We slow down, give up and go right back where we started. We go from A back to A.

Why does this happen? Could it be that while we set our destination, we don't plan our journey? Are weight loss targets simply about weighing yourself and choosing your desired 'magic number'? Is knowing where you want to go enough? Or are there other things you need to consider? Like, how you will get there, your exercise of choice, how you will make place for your new lifestyle.

And that's the point. You need to make room for weight loss, both in your life and in your mind. The proof – that you are indeed on the road to fitness – will be in the pudding that you are *not* eating, and in the healthy meals that you are.

Weight loss goals need to be both realistic and challenging. If you're a 35-year-old woman, have two kids (with the related responsibilities), 10-hour workdays, and you plan to lose 5 to 6 kilos a month, you are not only putting your own health at risk, you are also setting yourself up for feelings of failure and underachievement. Make it too easy for yourself, however, and you are far less likely to start off in the first place (there's always tomorrow, right?). Think about what you genuinely can manage. Because the key to *finishing* your weight loss journey is *starting* it right.

What follows in the next pages is an A to Z checklist designed to get you from your current weight (A) to your goal weight (B) in a way that allows you to be the architect of your own weight loss. By checking the boxes and filling in the blanks, you will automatically design the plan, the duration and figure out how weight loss can be woven into your lifestyle. This is *your* space, where I am going to give you the tools to correctly set targets customized to your convenience and to your need. Tick the boxes as you go through them one by one and get closer to fulfilling your unique weight loss needs.

First, the ABC

A. HOW MUCH DO YOU CURRENTLY WEIGH?

Weigh yourself first thing in the morning, preferably after you have gone to the loo (and cleared your bowels), before breakfast and in light clothes. This will be the lightest you will be in the day and is a fairly accurate estimate of your current weight.

If that's not possible, weigh yourself whenever you can. But no matter when you weigh yourself, track your progress by weighing yourself once a week on the same day, on the same weighing scale (different weighing scales are calibrated differently), at approximately the same time and in similar clothing (for example, if you weigh yourself in a salwar-kameez one week and in jeans the next, you will immediately weigh about half a kilo more).

Current weight _____ kilos
☐   Tick the box when done

B. PICK AN OUTFIT THAT WILL HELP YOU TRACK YOUR PROGRESS

No matter how closely you have followed your diet and how much you exercise, nobody shows results on the weighing scale every week. Pick out something from your existing wardrobe and use that as a marker for your weight loss progress. It could be a pair of jeans, a kurta, anything. If your clothes are getting looser and looser, or if you're fitting into something you haven't worn for years, you are losing weight, no matter what your weighing scale tells you.

☐ Tick the box when done

C. WHERE DO YOU WANT TO BE?

When setting a goal for yourself, always remember that you are one in a million! Your weight is unique to you and there is no one yardstick that fits everyone. It's great to have a goal to work towards, but one size – or, in this case, one magic number – doesn't fit all.

I don't believe in 'ideal' body weight, i.e., one weight for one height. I believe your ideal weight is the weight that suits you. Two men at 6 feet weighing in at 75 kilos will look different. For someone with a medium frame, it might be just perfect. If he is someone with a big frame, it might make him look quite thin. The key to effective goal setting is to pick a weight range, i.e., an outer and inner weight limit. In other words, you need to give yourself some room to wiggle.

LIC has devised a standard height-weight chart which prescribes weight ranges for Indian body types. It's an indication – you can be above it or below it if you wish. And please remember, there isn't any figure in the world (even according to height-weight charts) that says that if you are not at this number, you are not perfect.

Take a look at the height-weight chart and pick a weight range.

Height in metre and (feet/inches)	Men (in kilos)/pounds	Women (in kilos)/pounds
1.52 (5' 0")	–	50.8 to 54.4 / 112-120
1.54 (5' 1")	–	51.7 to 55.3 / 114-122
1.57 (5' 2")	56.3 to 60.3 / 124-133	53.1 to 56.7 / 117-125
1.60 (5' 3")	57.6 to 61.7 / 127-136	54.4 to 58.1 / 120-128
1.63 (5' 4")	58.9 to 63.5 / 130-140	56.3 to 59.9 / 124-132
1.65 (5' 5")	60.8 to 65.3 / 134-144	57.6 to 61.2 / 127-135
1.68 (5' 6")	62.2 to 66.7 / 137-147	58.9 to 63.5 / 130-140
1.70 (5' 7")	64.0 to 68.5 / 141-151	60.8 to 65.3 / 134-144
1.73 (5' 8")	65.8 to 70.8 / 145-156	62.2 to 66.7 / 137-147
1.75 (5' 9")	67.6 to 72.6 / 149-160	64.0 to 68.5 / 141-151
1.78 (5'10")	69.4 to 74.4 / 153-164	65.8 to 70.3 / 145-155
1.80 (5'11")	71.2 to 76.2 / 157-168	67.1 to 71.7 / 148-158
1.83 (6' 0")	73.0 to 78.5 / 161-173	68.5 to 73.9 / 151-163
1.85 (6' 1")	75.3 to 80.7 / 166-178	–
1.88 (6'2")	77.6 to 83.5 / 171-184	–
1.90 (6' 3")	79.8 to 85.7 / 176-189	–

(As compiled by the LIC of India and accepted as standard weight chart all over India. 'Height-Weight Chart for Indian Men and Women', http://www. mohanraohospital.com/heightweightchart.html, accessed on 31/3/2012)

Note:
Up to 30 years: 10 per cent above standard is acceptable.
Between 30 and 35 years: Standard is optimum weight.
Above 35 years: 10 per cent below standard is acceptable.

Weight range _____ **kilos**

☐   Tick the box when done

See what happens when you pick a range and not a single, rigid number? You are immediately reducing the pressure on yourself. You're recognizing that as long as you stay within the boundaries of your weight range, you are doing well. A single number is very difficult to stick to, in any case. Human bodies are not designed to be at the same weight every day of the week. In fact, your weight can fluctuate by up to 1 or 2 kilos in a single day – that's just basic human physiology. So why stick to something that eludes you?

When it comes to setting a weight loss goal for yourself, always remember that your goal is not set in stone. Weight loss is like money – you can always make more if you really want to. If you reach your weight range and feel like you still need to lose more, then by all means, do. But if you feel you look great at a higher weight and all your health indicators are fine, you don't need to weigh lower than that. You can stop whenever you want.

The D to Z of A to B

D. LOSE WEIGHT LIKE CLIMBERS CLIMB MOUNTAINS

If you're looking to lose 30 kilos, your goal should not be 'I want to lose 30 kilos'. Can you imagine losing a kilo and thinking, *OMG, 29 to go!* That's reason enough for anyone to give up! The moment you set your overall target, forget about it. Focus on new mini targets because if you break up your weight loss goal into bite-sized pieces, you are far more likely to achieve it.

Set your mini goals at three-month intervals. Three months give you enough time to set achievable targets. Every time you achieve that mini goal, your motivation levels will increase substantially. Studies show that in order to complete important tasks, we need to feel a sense of what is called self-efficacy, the belief that we have the skills and techniques necessary to succeed. Smaller targets help you build a strong sense of self-efficacy, which enables you to both reach and maintain your target weight.

It is not advisable to lose more than 2 to 4 kilos a month, so don't plan to lose more than 6 to 9 kilos every three months.

Do the math

- ❏ Number of kilos you need to lose as per your goal _____
- ❏ 2 to 3 kilos per month × 3 months = 6 to 9 kilos
- ❏ Total time needed to lose weight _____ months
  - ☐ Tick the box when done

MAKING SPACE FOR WEIGHT LOSS IN YOUR LIFE

Weight loss is as much about knowing what and how much to eat as about planning and organizing your life so that you can meet your goals. You need to have access to healthy food and exercise. You need to organize your existing system, or re-organize it so that you can accommodate your new lifestyle for the brief period that you are losing weight. While these are

organize your 'me' time

not massive changes, you do need to pay attention to four key parts: nutrition, exercise, your non-weight loss targets and managing your stress levels (i.e., planning your 'me' time).

Plan Your Nutrition

Since food is at the core of any good weight loss programme, find out if you are in a position to eat healthy. Tick the boxes as you go along.

ASK YOURSELF

E. Do you have access to healthy, fresh ingredients, fruits and vegetables?   ☐

F. Do you have good, non-stick cookware? ☐

G. Can you cook for yourself or can someone else cook healthy food for you in low oil? Do you have access to low-oil recipes? ☐

H. Can you spare 5 minutes a day to plan and organize your meals for the next day? ☐

I. How many glasses of water can you comfortably drink in a day? Circle one.   4 6 8 10 12

But what if you don't have access to a kitchen?

If you're a hostel resident or an executive living on your own with no access to a kitchen, you can still lose weight at a good pace. But hostel or canteen food is notoriously high in fat and swimming in oil, and there is no way you can lose weight effectively if you eat from these sources. I've heard of some wonderful solutions that my clients have come up with, just so they can stay on track. These include:

Dabba service

Many clients organize food from a dabba service for lunch and dinner with strict instructions to go easy on the oil and other diet specifications.

Resource buddy

An imaginative way to lose weight is to get a 'resource buddy'. Let's take the example of two college-going girls who come to me – Aditi and Aleysia. Aditi lives in a hostel and Aleysia lives at home. Both girls match their diets, i.e., they follow the same meal plan at the same time. Whenever Aleysia's mother cooks food for her daughter, she sends the same dabba for Aditi too. And it's working!

Lunch partner

This is another solution for busy working professionals. You and your lunch partner can take turns to bring lunch. You can match your diets and make sure the responsibility of cooking healthy food is shared. Simple but smart!

Not all food needs cooking

Whether it's bhel, hung-curd dip with cut veggies, a salad or a sandwich, not all healthy meals and snacks need to be cooked. You can make these wherever you are, and they are convenient, oil-free, take two minutes to prepare and are easy to carry. Other examples include cornflakes chaat, cornflakes or wheat flakes with milk or dahi, chhaas, veggies on crackers and dry poha chivda.

PLAN YOUR EXERCISE

If you haven't been exercising for years, aiming to show up at the gym six days a week is more than a little ambitious. Set yourself exercise goals that you are confident of achieving. Needless to say, how much exercise you fit into your schedule influences the rate at which you lose weight. Tick the boxes and fill in the blanks as you go along.

J.　Is there a gym close by or a walking track or any space where you can exercise regularly for an hour?　☐

K.　How many days a week can you exercise?
　　_____ days/ week　☐

If you can't spare a full hour for exercise, you can still lose weight by breaking up your 60 minutes into smaller exercise capsules. You could work out in six smaller sessions of 10 minutes each or even two sessions of 30 minutes each – whatever suits your time and convenience. Be the architect of your workout.

L. What time/ times can you fit this in?_____ a.m./ p.m. ☐

Take the timing you worked out on page 103. Fill it in here.

M. What needs to be done/ moved around to accommodate this
new exercise plan? ☐
- ❑ Can someone else drop the kids to school?
- ❑ Can you wake up an hour earlier?
- ❑ Can someone else take over house- or work-related
responsibilities for the hour that you will be out of the
house?
- ❑ Can you shift some of your responsibilities to weekends,
therefore clearing the week to walk?

N. How can you increase your levels of activity?
If you'd like see the kilos drop even faster, increase your
activity levels. Are there smaller distances you can walk? Can
you take the stairs? Can you walk to a colleague's desk instead
of emailing him? Can you do some of your own household
chores? Spare a few minutes to think about how you can
increase your burn by just going about your day. ☐

SET YOUR 'WEIGHTLESS' GOALS.
CHANGE THE QUALITY OF YOUR LIFE.

There is a phenomenon called Syndrome X, where multiple organs
suffer as a result of excessive weight gain. I have seen so many cases
where the client not only has lifestyle-related diseases like Type II
diabetes, but also has other conditions like heart disease and fatty
infiltration in the liver. Multiple organs, one cause.

Ideal body weight is to be looked at holistically. Focus on how
you want to feel. Apart from weight loss, set weightless targets so
that when you don't necessarily see the victories on the scale, you
stay motivated because you also have these other things to get

excited about. Tick the boxes on some common weight*less* targets, or use the space below to set some of your own.

O. I want to have more energy.   ☐

P. I want my clothes to fit better.   ☐

Q. I want to fall sick less often/ I want to reduce my medication. ☐

R. I want to play with my kids more/ participate more actively in life/ walk up the stairs without feeling breathless.   ☐

S. I want to have more confidence.   ☐

T. I want to have more control over my cravings.   ☐

U. I want to sleep better.   ☐

V. I want to be less irritable.   ☐

These are just examples. Keep coming back to this list to see how – and whether – the quality of your life has improved. You can use this space to set some of your own weightless targets.

My Weightless Goals

THE OTHER JOYS OF WEIGHT LOSS

When 82-year-old Mr Patel first walked into my clinic, he wasn't concerned about losing weight for the sake of losing it. He wasn't interested in fitting into nicer clothes or looking good. His objective was clear and simple:

'Pooja, I don't care about the weight. I don't care about what I am, what I should be, what I look like. I just don't care. All I care about is that I no longer have to walk with *this*.'

Propped against his chair was a walking stick. Mr Patel was dependent on it for all movement. It was his constant companion at dinners, birthday parties or at the park. He couldn't go anywhere without it. And he hated it. He was overweight, hypertensive, had diabetes, heart problems and a big belly. But he wasn't concerned about his health. He was concerned about his dignity.

His performance on my programme was a testament to how badly he wanted to let go of his crutch. He did brilliantly, losing a massive 25 kilos and faring as well as clients who were quarter his age. His health improved considerably and his medication was reduced to about half its quantity. And yes, ultimately, after eight months, he let go of that obvious reminder of his health – the walking stick.

Weight loss isn't always about looking good. What motivated a man in his eighties to do better than those less than half his age had more to do with improving the quality of his life. That's what kept him going. Mr Patel is an example I love to quote when I'm talking to clients who think that their efforts are only successful if they see the numbers go down. I always advise them to set their own weightless targets so that even if the scale doesn't match their expectations, their efforts take on a whole new meaning because they find joy in the other joys of weight loss.

Plan Your 'Me' Time

Stress can kill any good intention to get fitter. In the madness of our lives, we forget what we are eating, ignore meal times and often use food as a way to combat stress. If you want to stay on track with your weight loss, make a plan to manage your stress in ways that don't invite food as the chief guest. Engage in some sort of small relaxation activity, whether it's a hot bath, a massage, a trip to the spa, meditation or deep breathing. Unplug, disconnect, rejuvenate. Even if it's for just 15 or 20 minutes in a day, you won't feel that life overwhelms you.

W. I want to de-stress by _____   ☐

X. Time spent de-stressing _____ minutes/ day   ☐

Y. Evaluate your progress. Re-assess your weight loss goals at the end of three months and answer the following:

❑ Have you lost your 6 to 9 kilos?   ☐ Yes   ☐ No
❑ How many kilos did you lose in this period? _____
❑ Did you enjoy the journey?   ☐ Yes   ☐ No
❑ Do you feel a sense of achievement?   ☐ Yes   ☐ No
❑ How often did you exercise? _____ times a week
❑ How often did you eat out? _____ times a week
❑ How closely did you follow the meal plan?
    ❑   10–30 per cent
    ❑   30–50 per cent
    ❑   50–70 per cent
    ❑   70–100 per cent

Even if you didn't lose 6 to 9 kilos, and you lost 4 kilos, celebrate that. Studies suggest that even a 5 per cent decrease in your body weight leads to a reduction in medication (especially for those with diabetes and high blood pressure). Every kilo counts. And it's that much less you have to lose in the next three-month period!

Z. Remember you are special.   ☐

And finally, don't forget to tick this box to continually remind yourself that no matter how much weight you lose, or how much stress you are under, you are uniquely special and you are uniquely gorgeous. Treat your body with as much love as you would like to receive.

NUTRITION

At 45, she was one of the fittest MILs I had ever seen. Wearing leggings, a tank top with a jacket tied around her waist, Tanya Manchanda was my newest client. We got off to a great start.

'I have been to every dietician under the sun but nothing works. I'm sure you're very good... but I have no hope from you.'

What a great start.

Cases like Tanya's were not unfamiliar to me. She had lost almost all the weight she needed to, and only the last 6 kilos were left now. But owing to her slowing metab and the fact that she had already lost a considerable amount, she was, not surprisingly, finding the last few kilos the hardest to shed.

'I know you can't help me,' she continued, setting down her bag next to my measuring bowls, and leaning back in her chair. 'I'm just here to prove to you that you can't.'

I felt bad for her. No one – especially someone who looked this good – needed to be this upset about the last 6 kilometres of a distance she had run so well. But based on her blood tests and her eating habits, I made out a meal plan and told her to come back in four weeks.

She was back. And she hadn't lost a single gram.

'Pooja, you don't understand,' she said, close to tears now. 'I set alarms on my cell and ask the maids to remind me to eat every two hours. I eat bang on time, not a minute earlier or later. My vegetables and oil are monitored. Portion sizes are controlled. I went out and bought a set of bowls. I measure everything in the bowls. I weigh my food to make sure I eat exactly 100 grams per fruit or potato serving. I fill in my diary every day...'

I frowned a frown I usually reserve for those clients who have spent their weekends undoing the week's hard work. But I had no doubt that Tanya followed everything I outlined to the T. So why hadn't she lost weight?

She continued, 'I weigh myself first thing in the morning, before a bath, after a bath, before lunch, after lunch, before exercise, after exercise. And my weight has not budged. I've hired an expensive personal trainer to complement my diet. I can't sleep because I'm so stressed out by this. What more can I do? *It's not working!*'

She looked at me mournfully, her eyes filled with tears.

'I told you I'm never going to lose weight.'

When she told me how rigidly she followed my diet, I was impressed. But when she told me that she weighed herself *seven* times a day, I realized that Tanya didn't want to lose weight to look good or to feel better, she wanted to lose weight because she was obsessed with the *idea* of losing weight. She looked great for her age but she had an obsession with weight loss. For her, food equalled calories. For her, weight loss was not a way to get to her goal but it was the goal itself. So whenever she ate, her attitude was not 'I am fuelling my body and this tastes so good' but 'I am eating calories and I need to work this off at the gym'.

I spent the next 25 minutes talking to her. Even though I had a waiting room full of restless clients sitting outside, I had to understand why anyone would weigh themselves seven times a day. I told her that she had to enjoy the same food, without thinking about the calories. And just to prove to her that it was the attitude and not the diet, I asked her to follow the *same* plan with a happier, positive frame of mind. I told her to go out, have fun, do fun things. And she was not allowed to weigh herself at all.

Two weeks later, the same plan gave her fantastic results. Free from the leash of her weighing scale, she started to direct her energies elsewhere. She no longer drove her staff crazy. And in just 15 days, she lost the 2 kilos she had been struggling to lose for months. Same meal plan, two sets of attitudes.

Even though she eventually lost all 6 kilos, Tanya still comes over to my clinic to update me on her progress and to chat with clients in the waiting room about their weight loss. She's become an agony aunt of sorts and I always smile to myself when I overhear her counselling my clients in the waiting area, 'Don't worry, don't obsess over it. Just let it go, and even your weight will go.'

Just let it go. Just let it go. Just let it go.

JUST LET IT GO

Obsession is as unhealthy as a crash diet. Tanya's story illustrates the point I was making earlier –this is the only body you have. Learn to love it and appreciate it. Don't sweat the little things and stop obsessing over every single calorie. The results will come. For some, they come faster. For some, they take a little time. But there is *no* way that eating healthy will not make you reach your weight loss goals. Remember that.

FAT BALANCE

This is something many of my clients experience towards the end of their programme: just as they get to the absolute end of their weight loss, the last bit becomes too hard to shed. This can be really demotivating for someone who has spent months – and, in some cases, years – to get to his or her goal weight.

The first thing I tell them is, relax and trust your body: you *will* get there (and I've always been proved right about this!). The second thing I do is to ask them to think of this phenomenon as money in the bank – the more money you have, the more you can withdraw, right? In the same way, the greater the amount of fat, the more 'withdrawals' you can make from your 'fat account'. So when you are 15 to 20 kilos overweight, you can lose 3 to 5 kilos a month. But when you have just 3 to 5 kilos to go, it will be slower. You won't lose more than 2 to 3 kilos a month (or less), even if you watch what you eat and exercise regularly.

The less you have, the less you can lose because you don't have that much more to 'withdraw'. If the last bit is taking time, don't lose heart: it just means that you're almost there.

The Diet Jungle

Tanya had gone to so many dieticians and fitness experts that she used to joke that she had enough for the star cast of her own TV show. According to the latest estimates, the global market for weight loss is expected to cross US$586 billion by the year 2014.[8] Wherever you go, there are people selling everything from diet pills to cellulite creams, self-help books to lectures, seminars and retreats. Everyone's buying into the newest, hottest quick fix faster than the products hit the shelves. From housewives in Chandigarh to teenagers in Kochi, everyone seems to want to Lose. Weight. Now.

---

[8] 'Global Market for Weight Loss Worth US$586.3 Billion by 2014', http://www.marketsandmarkets.com/PressReleases/global-market-for-weight-loss-worth-$726-billion-by-2014.asp, accessed on 28/1/12

I'm not saying that the products will not make you lose weight as advertised. They will do what they promise – make you thin. But if that's your only goal, you need to ask yourself a few questions: What good is becoming a size zero if it means you can't have a baby? How good does your new body feel if you squeeze into a bikini at the same time as you slide into depression? And what good is being thin if you're at an increased risk of prostate cancer, malnutrition, osteoporosis, heart disease and even death?

The Diet Jungle is a mad, crazy jungle. And like in every jungle, there are hunters looking to make a fast buck. I have treated hundreds of clients who have come to me after going through diets that no human body is designed to follow. Based on my clients' experiences and my own research, I have broadly classified some of the world's most popular – and risky – diets into categories so that you can recognize some of the more damaging – and short-term – ways to lose weight. Blow the whistle if you spot the following 'animals'.

THE CAMEL

What I call Camel Diets are those which make you drink like a camel. High on liquids, these diets make you drink, drink, drink and drink. I had a client who came to me fresh off a high liquid diet in which she was made to drink lime shots, eat very little and consume 4 litres of water every day. *Every day.* The question you should ask yourself is not how much weight you can lose on one of these diets. The question you should ask yourself is: between running to the fridge and running to the bathroom, do you have time for anything else?

Seriously, though, when you go on a high liquid diet, you are in danger of malnutrition. In this kind of diet, water is used to keep the stomach filled. Your hunger pangs are caused by the peristaltic movements in your stomach, and these peristaltic movements –

which sometimes make your stomach growl – give you the signal to go look for food. By drinking so much water, you are suppressing your hunger signals. So while you might feel full, you're not eating much and your body is slowly sliding into starvation mode. And while you're suppressing your hunger signals, your body is sending you others, in the form of short-term side effects. These include dizziness, breathlessness, headaches, hallucinations, nausea, low blood pressure, palpitations and extreme fatigue.

If you are drinking – and not eating – your way through weight loss, you will be almost completely deprived of carbohydrates, proteins, fats, vitamins and minerals. All liquid diets are crash diets and are additionally associated with hair loss, brittle nails, weaker bones, weaker teeth, weaker digestive tracts, irritable bowels and long-term muscle degeneration.

And that's not all. Drinking 4 litres of water a day had taken a toll on my client. Her weight was yo-yo'ing so badly and her metabolism had slowed down to such an extent that it took ages for her to take it up to the normal rate for her age and height. And nothing can prevent the weight from coming back. The moment you stop drinking and start eating, the weight will definitely – and rapidly – return.

What a Camel Looks Like

Examples include all detox diets, the 'Orange Juice Diet' or the 'Master Cleanse'. If your diet is unbalanced in favour of liquids, it's time to step out of the pond.

WARM WATER WITH LIME?
WASTE OF TIME.

The 'lime with warm water' rule is one of the biggest misconceptions in the dieting world and it's amazing how many people think it's a healthy thing to do. Many feel that if they start their day with warm water and lime, it helps burn fat and lose weight. But that's not true. Like grapefruit, lime has no proven capability of burning fat. In fact, lime with warm water has been associated with leeching or extracting calcium from the bones, possibly leading to osteoporosis. And while there have been no significant studies to back this theory, I personally find that most of my clients who drink lime with warm water have correspondingly low serum (i.e., circulating blood level) calcium.

But does this mean you can't have fresh lime soda or nimbu paani? No, far from it. Water at room temperature or cold water with lime does not have the same effect as warm water and lime. This is because, at a warmer temperature, the mixture causes a change in cellular osmolarity. Osmolarity refers to the direction in which calcium ions move. With warm water and lime, calcium ions are thought to move from the bones into the blood (which weakens the bones and increases the risk of osteoporosis) as opposed to the other way round from the blood into the bones.

THE MONKEY

Monkey Diets jump from fad to fad, from acai berries to apple cider vinegar. Whatever is shiny and new, the Monkey will take some of it, discard part of it, and retain whatever's convenient. Monkey Diets will give you half-baked information about a particular 'new' food and place too much emphasis on its benefits. One ingredient will dominate the diet and it's just too much of a good thing.

The Grapefruit Diet, a diet that has never gone out of style, is a classic example of a Monkey. The idea behind the diet is that grapefruit has an enzyme that burns fat. However, while this is yet to be proven conclusively even after all these years (the diet has been around since the 1930s), the Grapefruit Diet has an overall calorie count that is far too low to be maintained in the long run.

While grapefruit is a wonderful source of Vitamin C, fibre and other disease-fighting agents, it is not by itself a solution to fat loss or weight loss.

Things have changed since the 1930s and fad diets have become weirder, and far more dangerous. I came across something called the Cotton Ball Diet, in which you swallow cotton balls to lose weight! They fill up the space in your stomach, and you don't feel hungry as often. The idea behind it is that since cotton is a plant it'll eventually get digested by your system. *Cotton balls!* Are you serious?!

And have you heard of the HCG Diet?[9] HCG – or Human Chorionic Gonadotropin – is a prescribed treatment for infertility. Weight loss candidates are injected with HCG and given a 500 calorie diet to go with it. As it is supposed to help with fertility, these injections 'fool' the body into thinking it is pregnant, and the body in turn proceeds to burn fat just as it would if there was a baby growing inside. Those who endorse this diet claim that women lose a pound a day without feeling hungry. It's great, as long as you avoid the small print which indicates major side effects. As a nutritionist, I get furious when I read these things. How can people take chances like this with their health?

But the hands-down craziest one so far is the Tapeworm Diet. Here, dieters have to swallow tapeworms (which are living, breathing parasites, by the way). Once in the stomach, the tapeworms eat the food, so that you can continue eating as much as you like. Yuck! And what if the tapeworm gets bored and decides to travel to other parts of the body, like the brain? People always tell me they are dying to lose weight, but in this case they just might.

---

[9] 'Reality Check: Weight Loss Shots', http://blog.foodnetwork.com/healthyeats/ 2011/05/10/reality-check-weight- loss-shots/, accessed on 15/1/12

Taking a Trip on a Monkey

While the above are extreme examples of fads gone wrong, when you follow a Monkey Diet, you are going on diets that promote one key food group at the cost of another. No one ingredient or food group should ever dominate a diet because it will always do so at the expense of something your body needs. And what you need is a balance of macronutrients (proteins, carbs, fats) and micronutrients (vitamins and minerals) for sustained and healthy weight loss.

Smelling a Monkey

The best way to identify a Monkey Diet is if the diet uses the key ingredient in its title: for example, the Grapefruit Diet or the Apple Cider Vinegar Diet. This already means that there is too much emphasis on that particular food. You should think of the ideal weight loss plan as a Bollywood multi-starrer like *Golmaal 3* or *Phir Hera Pheri* – you don't want to place too much focus on one hero!

THE COW

The next time you're in a lush green meadow – or at a traffic signal – notice how cows eat. Cows keep chewing on the same thing for hours and hours. No variety, just the same thing day in and day out. Cow Diets are almost like Monkey Diets except that they don't just have one ingredient as the key component, they are almost fully composed of one recurring ingredient. In other words, that is all you are allowed to eat.

The Cabbage Soup Diet is all about cabbage. And soup. It's a seven-day diet and involves copious amounts of the same foods. Day 1 doesn't look very different from Day 7 and the total calorie count will rarely exceed 1000 calories. Whichever way you look at it, this kind of diet is severely restrictive.

But we shouldn't just look to the West for diets like this. Cows can be found closer home. Kanika came in looking for a change in her diet. And soon I found out why. When we were discussing the diet she was currently on, the conversation went something like this:

What do you have for breakfast?

'Boiled moong dal sprouts and tea.'

Lunch?

'Moong dal ki roti with moong dal tikki.'

And do you have dal with that?

'Yeah. Moong dal.'

What do you do at teatime?

'Boiled moong dal sprouts.'

And dinner?

'Same as lunch. Moong dal ki roti with moong dal tikki. But for variation, I also have dessert...'

Thank goodness, I thought to myself. At least she's breaking out of her rut.

And what do you have for dessert?

'Moong dal halwa.'

Oh, god.

Kanika was given her diet by an Ayurvedic doctor who told her that a diet of only moong dal was the ultimate cure for weight gain. She also had to cook everything in cow's ghee (not buffalo ghee) because she was told that cow's ghee was not fattening! This poor girl was not allowed to eat fruit, vegetables, or much else. It was just moong, moong and more moong. And it's not that this diet was making her look tired. She had good energy levels and she looked happy (two things I look for when I meet a new client) but she was complaining of 'thoda joint pain'.

The minute she said 'joint pain', I asked her to bring her blood reports and get a serum uric acid test done. When I took a look at her results, I found that her uric acid levels had gone through the roof! Serum uric acid levels for a woman her age should have been nothing above 5.5. Her level was 8.

When you have excess protein by eating purine-rich foods like dal, red meat or alcohol (purines are by-products of protein metabolism), it leads to the formation of excess uric acid (hyperuricemia), and this excess uric acid has nowhere to go. So what does it do? It slowly begins to store itself in the smaller joints of your body, and you start getting aches and pains, which could lead to gout. And this is just one side effect of excess protein. Too much protein is also associated with kidney problems, osteoporosis, cancer and obesity.

This is just an example of a high-protein Cow Diet. You could have a diet where you eat only raw veggies or fruit, for example, and your body will suffer in different ways.

The second point I want to make is that variety is incredibly important in eating healthy and you will never sustain any diet if it's too restrictive and if it limits your eating options to such an extent. Bear in mind that the key to sticking to any successful weight loss plan is to dress it up and provide substitutes.

Hearing the Moo

If you're eating the same thing for breakfast, lunch and dinner, you've become a cow. Even if you feel full, please remember that your body is being deprived of vital nutrients and this is also a kind of malnutrition.

THE OSTRICH

While they target weight loss, these diets bury their head in the sand and don't address your overall health. What they do – and do very well – is address the issue of weight loss. You will always lose weight on an Ostrich Diet. But a lot of the time, your health will take the hit.

While all the diets I have discussed above do nothing for your general well-being and can also be called Ostrich Diets, the best example of an Ostrich is the Atkins Diet because it appears healthy and is easily misunderstood. When it first came on the scene, the no-carbs rule was seen as the superstar of diets. The diet allowed you to have cheese, red meat, ice-cream and whatever else you wanted. How amazing is that!

Since then, the Atkins Diet has been widely discredited. You will lose weight, yes, but you will lose a lot more than that. Atkins dieters have been associated with being at an increased risk of breast cancer, heart disease, prostate cancer and kidney problems. They also get less blood flow to their most important organs[10] like the brain and heart which may also lead to sexual dysfunction.

Do the Atkins for two months and I can show you the effects of the diet. Your (before–after) blood reports will read like two different people. Your triglycerides, SGPT* levels, uric acid levels, LDL cholesterol (bad cholesterol) will go through the roof, because the focus is high fat and high protein. In fact, in the Atkins Diet there is unlimited fat and unlimited protein.

Getting Your Head Out of the Sand

The simplest way to identify an Ostrich Diet is if it ignores vital food groups: macronutrients like carbs and fats or micronutrients like vitamins and minerals. If you want your weight loss plan to work, you have to get your head out of the sand.

---

[10] Dean Ornish, *Eat More, Weigh Less*, Quill, 2001

* SGPT (Serum Glutamic Pyruvic Transaminase) is an enzyme that is usually present in liver and heart cells. When there is damage to the liver or the heart, SGPT is released into the blood.

THE CHEETAH

These are my favourite diets for sheer entertainment value. Cheetahs are the fastest runners in the animal kingdom and can run at speeds of 70 miles per hour. Cheetah Diets are those in a rush, which promise magical time frames. Where you will be in the best shape of your life and fit into your college jeans in 30 days. These claims are usually followed by four magic words: Or your money back.

A Cheetah Leaves the Following Footprints

❏ 5 kilos in 20 days. Or your money back.
❏ Lose up to 16 kilos/ 30 inches in less than three months. Or your money back.
❏ Drop 3 kilos in 72 hours for your wedding! Or your money back.
❏ Lose 8 kilos in two months and don't get out of your house – lose weight on the phone! Or your money back.

I have a client who went to a 'spa' for two weeks, where she was actually made to vomit food out of her body to 'cleanse' her system. They had to purge the 'bad food' from her body because it was thought to be toxic. They went to the extent of washing her colon with water to remove the toxins. Why? Because some foods are clearly your enemy. She lost 5 kilos in those two weeks, as promised. Hurray. So what if her body went through trauma because of all the puking? Like cricket scores or petrol mileage, it all boils down to the number, right?

Unfortunately, there are no shortcuts to weight loss and I really wish I could tell you differently. If your body experiences fast weight loss (i.e., exceeding a kilo a week), you will probably gain it all back. Cheetah Diets go nowhere. And you will get nowhere fast.

THE SLOTH

Where cheetahs rush in, sloths fear to tread. Moving at the rate of 6 feet per minute in some cases, sloths are the slowest movers in the animal kingdom and are found mostly in the forests of Central and South America. The Sloth Diet is the laziest way to lose weight.

This kind of weight loss is an 'animal' of a different kind and doesn't involve crash-dieting or too many fluids. Here you don't have to *do* anything – a machine does it for you. Electrical Muscle Stimulation or EMS is a vibrating machine that passively stimulates your BMR. To lose weight, all you have to do is lie down. With their vibrating action, EMS machines create muscular movements the same way exercise does and will not only help with weight loss but will also bump up your BMR.

I've treated hundreds of clients who have used EMS. In many cases, they have fully gained back all the weight they had lost in about the same time they took to lose it. The difficulty with these machines is that they don't help you make dietary or exercise changes. So the moment you stop using EMS, the benefits subside, your BMR comes down again and the weight loss is effectively reversed. Because to maintain the effects of EMS, you need to continue exercising.

When you're in the 'weight loss' mode and you're eating healthy and exercising regularly, you are in that 'mindset' of weight loss: you are geared to make lifestyle changes. But if you continue to have your samosa with Coke at 5 p.m. every day and then lie down on a machine to help you work it off, you 'outsource' your weight loss to a machine, and you will never alter your lifestyle. Most people who use these machines are not used to exercising to keep up the weight loss because a commitment to lying down and a commitment to going for a walk are very different. And when you don't make lifestyle changes, any weight loss plan – be it mine or someone else's – will *always* be temporary.

Look at it this way. The time spent is the same – one hour. Instead of spending 60 minutes lying down to make a machine work on your muscles, use that same hour to get the benefits of actual exercise, which has been medically documented as a cure for more than just excess weight. Because if you really want long-term weight loss, you need to challenge your body. You have to *go* to exercise instead of waiting for exercise to *come* to you.

NOW YOU SEE IT, NOW YOU DON'T

'No diet! No exercise! Lose weight with massage!' Ever wonder what that's all about? Well, this phenomenon consists of a little bit of 'magic'.

A client of mine signed up for a six-month programme in which she was asked to limit her fluid intake (including water, tea, coffee, milk, etc) to a litre a day. She was then massaged with 'special imported creams'. After every massage session, there was magic! She had lost inches in *minutes*.

Sounds too good to be true? Unfortunately, it is. What looks like instantaneous inch loss actually uses dehydration to achieve quick results. The creams used for the massages suck water from the skin. Naturally, after one sitting, your skin will be suppressed and you will immediately 'lose' inches. Besides, if you drink less, as my client was instructed to do, you will weigh less anyway.

Secondly, if weight loss depends on dehydration for results, it will reverse the moment you start hydrating yourself. Water will return to its rightful place in the connective tissues of your skin and the inches will reappear as magically as they disappeared. Now you see inch loss. Now you don't.

SO IF THE DIET JUNGLE IS ABOUT HOW NOT TO LOSE WEIGHT, HOW SHOULD SKINNY FEEL?

In 2009, British supermodel Kate Moss famously said that 'nothing tastes as good as skinny feels'. She was widely condemned for encouraging anorexia, bulimia and other eating disorders. While the debate raged on with regard to the impact of her comments on young teenage girls, I'd like to focus on the second part of her comment. How should skinny feel?

Skinny should always, always feel good and none of the 'animals' in the Diet Jungle will make you feel that way. Your weight loss plan should make you feel like you have a weight lifted off your shoulders and not just your scale. You should be active, happy and looking to the future. That's when you know you are on the right track. And when I see a happy, smiling client with colour in her cheeks, I know I'm on the right track.

In the ensuing pages, I will give you a complete guide to losing weight by using the most important weapon in your arsenal: food. So many of my clients have stopped or reduced taking their hypertension/ hypothyroid/ diabetes medication after following their meal plan. And it's not because I'm a magician. It is simply because that's the power of the food we eat. Forget just obesity, the right food in the right proportions is capable of tackling heart disease, diabetes, hypertension, depression and even cancer. Garlic, tomatoes, broccoli, soya, green tea, dark chocolate all have cancer-fighting properties and weight loss is just a happy by-product. In other words, you can find nourishment on your plate and not just inside a pill.

On your plate lies the answer to so many issues plaguing your life – from the mental to the physical. Your plate holds not just fuel for your system. It carries all the tools you need to do more with your body and your life than you have ever done. Because food is not just fuel. Food is power.

The Active Phase

There are two phases in my programme: active and passive. The Active Phase is when your body sheds weight and the diets and exercises you follow are designed exclusively for weight loss. The Passive Phase is dedicated to a long-term maintenance plan with a view to ensuring that the weight stays off for life.

But I don't want to immediately launch into what to eat and what not to eat. Before embarking on your race to the finish line, I want to prepare you with a few facts on effective weight loss. ON YOUR MARKS... will tell you what you should be looking for in a weight loss plan to ensure that you are doing it the right way. GET SET... will educate you about key nutrients your body simply cannot do without. And EAT! is what you've all been waiting for: diets and nutritional guides. You will be surprised at how much you can eat and how much you will lose by eating things you never thought you could.

So what are you waiting for? Let the journey begin.

On Your Marks...

SANTA CLAUS YOUR WEIGHT LOSS

Before I prescribe what to eat, I want to talk a little more about what to expect from your weight loss plan. Treat your weight loss plan like Santa Claus. Expect things from it. Remember how you used to wait for Santa at the Christmas party in your building or school? (Of course, years later you realized Santa was actually your best friend's dad, but that's another story). You expected cool things from Santa – the latest board games, Barbie dolls, GI Joe, a shiny new cycle. You have to expect things from your diet as well.

Asking for just weight loss is like asking Santa for a kite or a pencil or a sharpener. Anyone can give you that. You don't need Santa. But if you're going to take control of your weight, if you're going to make changes in the way you eat, shouldn't you expect better returns on your diet?

Four Gifts You Should Ask Santa for

1. Dear Santa: Permanent weight loss

If you choose a diet that focuses only on losing weight, then it will ignore other issues like metabolism and overall health. Your diet needs to guarantee permanent weight loss, where the weight does not come back if you eat normally.*

2. Dear Santa: Increased metabolism

A good diet should kickstart your metabolism and actually increase it. Eating every two hours is the secret to stable weight loss. When my clients burst through the door telling me, 'I lost 3 kilos!', I am never impressed. The first question I ask them is, 'Did you eat every two hours?' Because without that, I know (from my experience with all my clients) that the 3 kilos are going to come back.

3. Dear Santa: Fat loss

If you don't lose fat, you lose muscle. And the more muscle you lose, the higher your body fat percentage becomes, which in turn leads to the storage of more fat. Any meal plan that is low on calories and basically starves you will ensure that your body uses muscle for its daily functioning, which is detrimental to any long-term weight loss goal.

* As long as you follow the rules of the maintenance plan

4. Dear Santa: Overall health, energy and well-being

How are you *feeling*? This is something no weighing scale or blood test will be able to tell you. Do you get up in the morning and feel lively and full of energy? Do you want to suddenly try new things or get more active? Do you find yourself walking more? Do you feel that you have a better attention span? Do you feel less angry or less irritable?

Your energy levels should remain more or less the same throughout the day: there should be no major highs or lows, where you're buzzing around one moment and flopping down on the couch the next. You blood sugar levels should be consistent and stable. Your overall health and well-being is the ultimate test of the success of any weight loss programme, and when you feel this way, you know you are losing it the right way.

Get Set...

THE FIVE FINGERS OF WEIGHT LOSS

Remember those 'United we stand, divided we fall' ads that used to play on DD? Those cute little short films about the importance of unity? The funda was simple: five fingers by themselves will not be effective unless you close your fingers and make a fist. That simple action gives you power.

It's a classic example and the simplest way to explain the principles of balanced nutrition. By themselves, the Five Fingers of Weight Loss – proteins, carbohydrates, fats, vitamins and minerals – have their 'own function but the various nutrients must act in unison for effective action'.[11] In other words, for long-lasting weight loss, you need to close your fingers and make a fist. Eat all five nutrients. Every day. There is no better way.

---

[11] S.R. Mudambi and M.V. Rajagopal, *Fundamentals of Food, Nutrition and Diet Therapy*, New Age International Publishers, 2009

The Five Fingers of Weight Loss can further be broken down into three macronutrients (proteins, carbs, fats) and two micronutrients (vitamins, minerals), and the reason it is divided in this way is because it represents the relative importance on your plate. Don't go overloading your vitamins at the cost of carbs or cutting fats and going crazy about protein. Absence – or too much emphasis – of any one nutrient will not only compromise your health but also result in short-term gains, sending you right back where you started.

Collectively, these five nutrients are your defence against disease, obesity, heart attacks and almost anything else you need to defend yourself against. Diabetes? Make a fist. Heart disease? Hey, you've got your fist. Obesity? Talk to the fist, baby! So many diseases are lifestyle-related and can be eradicated – not just improved – by making a proper fist. Read on, then, so that you can get the true benefits of a power-packed punch.

Fats

This poor nutrient has been treated like a criminal who has been tried and tested and hung without a fair trial. Fats have been defended by terrible lawyers, and have always been subjected to cruel and unnecessary punishment. Please note that fats are not micronutrients, they are macronutrients, which puts them in the same league as proteins and carbs, and they are a key nutrient for your body. You *cannot* – and I can't emphasise this enough –do without this incredibly crucial component. So no non-fat diet is ever going to work for you without having a negative impact on your overall health.

Fats play a huge role in protecting your vital organs. Your brain, heart and liver are all protected by a layer of fat and water. Fat is a bad conductor of heat. That's good news for you, because fat rests right beneath your skin, regulating your body temperature and keeping you warm and comfortable. Your nerves are guarded by fat. Your joints are lubricated by fat so that you can move around easily. And fat also helps in the absorption of vitamins A, D, E and K.

For those of you who want to reduce your body fat percentage, please remember that fat burning itself is a high-metabolic activity and can only be done at its optimum level when all your systems are functioning properly. Your body needs to be fuelled by the appropriate amount of carbs, proteins, vitamins, minerals *and* fats in order to set the stage for effective fat loss. Quite simply, you need fats to cut fat.

But if it's so good for us, why is it so bad for us? Well, it's the classic case of punishing the whole class just because of a few naughty boys.

GOOD FATS: THE 'MONOPOLY'

MUFA

If you're going mad over good fats versus bad fats, simply go nuts. Nuts (specifically peanuts, walnuts, almonds and pistachios), avocado, canola oil, safflower oil and olive oil, are excellent sources of Monounsaturated Fatty Acids (MUFA). While MUFAs lower 'bad' cholesterol and increase 'good' cholesterol, they have been found to aid weight loss, particularly fat loss. They also aid in maintaining the cells in your body and are by and large high in Vitamin E.

PUFA

Polyunsaturated Fatty Acids (PUFAs) lower your overall cholesterol. These fats aren't made by the body but are nevertheless essential fats that your body needs. You can find PUFAs in seafood like salmon, in fish oil, and in safflower oil, sunflower oil, soy and corn. Found in vegetables and fish oils, the life-giving Omega 3 and Omega

Nutrition Facts	
Serving Size 1 bag 7 oz 198g (198 g)	
Amount Per Serving	
Calories 972	Calories from Fat 558
	% Daily Value*
Total Fat 64g	99%
Saturated Fat 16g	80%
Trans Fat	
Cholesterol 0mg	0%
Sodium 1485mg	62%
Total Carbohydrate 105g	35%
Dietary Fiber 9g	35%
Sugars	
Protein 15g	

6 fatty acids – which aid the development of your brain and help keep your body healthy – are also part of the PUFA group.

There's a term I came across once which will help you remember the essential fats your body needs. The term is 'Monopoly' (Mono+Poly). Your diet needs a monopoly of fats in order for you to lose weight and achieve your health goals.

> **Label Guide**: Look out for MUFAs and PUFAs on the nutritional label when you go grocery shopping. The total fat consumed by you in the course of the day should not be less than 10 per cent of your daily calorie requirement or approximately 20 grams (based on a 2000 calorie diet).

BAD FATS

Saturated Fats

Found in meat, full-fat dairy products, egg yolk and in some plant sources including coconut oil, palm kernel oil, palm oil and cottonseed oil, saturated fats are fats that occur naturally. While the body does use these fats for its structural and physiological functions,[12] it makes enough of its own saturated fats to meet those needs. Therefore, you don't need to consume them from an external source. The WHO, in association with the United States Centers for Disease Control (CDC) and Food and Drug Administration (FDA), has asked people to reduce their intake of saturated fats due to their linkages with high cholesterol, coronary heart disease and stroke.

Trans Fats

Invented by scientists, trans fats are a completely man-made problem and are the result of the process of 'hydrogenation' of liquid oils. Trans fats were created solely to ensure that food lasted longer on the shelves. When you ingest trans fats, trans fatty acids are formed inside your body, which are extremely hazardous to your health. Found in many commercially packaged foods, they have been associated with heart disease, Alzheimer's, cancer, diabetes, depression, infertility in women and, of course, obesity. Besides, trans fats have negligible nutrient value. But

don't worry about spotting these bad boys. Because of the health risks, companies have no choice but to indicate the presence of trans fats in a product. All you have to do is watch out for it.

> **Label Guide:** Please avoid all products with trans fat content. In fact, more often than not, products will indicate that they are free of trans fats. And while you should ideally avoid saturated fats altogether, if you do consume them, they should never exceed 3 grams per day.

[12] *American Dietary Guidelines*, 2010, http://www.cnpp.usda.gov/Publications/ DietaryGuidelines/2010/PolicyDoc/PolicyDoc.pdf, accessed on 2/2/12

Proteins

If fats have been tried and punished and sentenced to death, proteins have been defended by some kickass lawyers, who have done great things for their brand image. And rightly so. Proteins are incredibly important for your body and you require them on a daily basis. Most people think proteins are required for kids trying to grow taller, or if you're training with weights. But no human body can function without protein.

The main function of protein is tissue building and it is also vital to the replacement of worn-out cells during the regular wear and tear of the body. Proteins transport life-giving substances throughout the body, produce valuable enzymes, hormones, anti-bodies and neurotransmitters, and are invaluable when it comes to growth and repair. They also build muscle. If you deprive yourself of adequate protein, you can suffer from hair loss, brittle nails, and weak bones and teeth. Drastic effects include reduced immunity, loss of muscle mass, growth failure, weakening of the heart and respiratory system and, in some cases, even death.

To make protein, you need amino acids, also known as the 'building blocks of protein'. In other words, proteins form inside our body as a result of amino acids 'bonding' with each other. We need 22 of these amino acids, but our bodies produce only 13. The other 9 – known as EAAs or essential amino acids – are obtained through foods like dal, nuts, seeds, eggs, chicken, meat and soya.

However, only some foods contain all the amino acids required to build new protein. These foods are called 'complete proteins' and mostly animal sources of protein (meats, eggs, etc) tend to be complete. Vegetarians, please note that plant sources like dal don't contain the 9 essential amino acids. So, dal is still an 'incomplete' source of protein. The best way to 'complete' it is to combine two plant protein sources. For example,

Nutrition Facts	
Serving Size 1 bag 7 oz 198g (198 g)	
Amount Per Serving	
Calories 972	Calories from Fat 558
	% Daily Value*
Total Fat 64g	99%
Saturated Fat 16g	80%
Trans Fat	
Cholesterol 0mg	0%
Sodium 1485mg	62%
Total Carbohydrate 105g	35%
Dietary Fiber 9g	35%
Sugars	
Protein 15g	
Vitamin A 9% • Vitamin C	112%
Calcium 10% • Iron	21%
*Percent Daily Values are based on a 2,000 calorie diet. Your daily values may be higher or lower depending on	

dal should be eaten with rice in order to accumulate all 9 essential amino acids. Other plant sources of protein include grains, pulses and nuts. Therefore, to get their dose of all amino acids needed to make new protein – and to keep the body's systems in good shape – vegetarians should eat a variety of protein-rich foods each day. However, two dals or two sets of grains cannot be combined and need to be alternated, preferably.

It's so tempting to bask in the glow of all the good press protein gets. Proteins make your digestive system work its butt off simply because your body needs more calories to digest protein. Additionally, they slow down the movement of food from your stomach to your intestine, which is why you feel fuller for longer. On an average, they spike your metabolic rate by a massive 30 per cent as opposed to just 4 per cent for carbs or fats. This is what makes high-protein diets so popular. I'm not going to go into how overdosing on this nutrient is detrimental to your health. But I will say this: you cannot go high-protein without going low-carb

THE 'NO DAL' GIRL

Once upon a time, there was a girl who didn't eat dal...

...Okay, I'll ditch the storytelling format. But let me tell you about this 25-year-old girl who came to my clinic. She had got married recently and was desperately trying to conceive, with no luck. She had been subjected to multiple infertility treatments and was pumped with progesterone and all sorts of hormones. She was bloated, puffed up and had come to me because her doctors had asked her to lose weight if she wanted to conceive. Ironically, it was the infertility treatments that made her gain weight in the first place.

During her diet recall, while discussing what she ate during the day, she had me completely stumped. She didn't eat dal! She hated it. In fact, she hated it so much that – barring a few exceptions as a child – she had never eaten dal in her life! I couldn't believe it! I was shocked. I was just about to start typing out her meal plan but my fingers hovered uncertainly over the keyboard, wondering what to do next.

What's the big deal, you ask. The big deal is that she was a vegetarian and she didn't eat dal. So if she didn't eat meat and she didn't eat eggs, where was she getting her protein from?

I asked her about the texture of her hair. She said that while she used to have good hair, it had become brittle, thin and was not growing longer. I asked her how her nails were. She said she always kept them short, because if she grew them, they started chipping. And these were just the visible side effects. When I analysed her serum protein levels, they were – unsurprisingly – markedly lower than normal. She had acne. Her ovulation levels were so low that doctors could not perform infertility treatments because her body was not producing enough eggs. How could it? If her body was unable to sustain itself, how could it go into reproductive mode? Her doctors should have analysed her diet before starting infertility procedures. Or at least someone should have asked her what she ate. But nobody did.

I pumped her up with dal. I gave her three bowls of dal per day. We were both amazed at the results. She had energy, stamina and was genuinely happy for the first time in years. She couldn't believe she was the same person. And her story had a 'happily ever after': twelve months after making nutritional changes, 'No dal' girl gave birth to a healthy baby boy.

or low-fat. And when your diet is based on depriving yourself of at least one or two out of the five essential nutrients, it won't be long before your body starts to show it.

STRIVE FOR EGG-CELLENCE

If you could make me the brand ambassador for any one thing, it would be for the egg white. I love the egg white – both eating it and prescribing it. It's one of the most important parts of my programme for my non-vegetarian clients because it is easily one of the best sources of protein around and is packed to the absolute brim with the goodness of both vitamins and minerals. It's a remarkable food because each egg white is not only low calorie (16 calories) but gives you a massive 4 grams of unmatched protein. In other words, it's not just about the quantity, it's about quality. And it is a 100 per cent reference protein, which means that all the protein it contains can be fully absorbed by your body, without any valuable protein getting lost in translation.

I do prescribe egg yolks to my clients but it's usually in the maintenance part of my programme. While you don't need to rule it out entirely, the yolk of the egg is still a source of both saturated fat and cholesterol and you may need to mellow the yellow if you want to get – and stay – fit.

Label Guide: Unlike MUFA, PUFA, saturated and trans fats which are all 'avatars' of fat and need to be carefully checked, proteins are indicated clearly on all nutritional labels. The average daily intake is calculated as 0.8 to 1 gram per kilo per ideal body weight. So if your ideal body weight (corresponding to your height) is in the range of 46 to 57 kilos, you need to eat 46 to 57 grams of protein per day (approx).

Foods can either be good, average or poor sources of protein. If 100 grams of food is composed of 10 grams of protein (or 10 per cent), it is considered a good source of protein. However, if the food is constituted of 5 to 10 per cent or less than 5 per cent protein, it is considered an average or poor source of protein respectively.

Carbohydrates

When I prescribe meal plans containing the recommended doses of carbs, my clients look at me like I've gone mad.

'You mean I can have rice?'

'Bread? Every day? What sort of diet is this?'

And then the disbelief is replaced by fear.

'Potatoes? But I have diabetes.'

'So many rotis? Are you sure about this? It doesn't sound right.'

Like fats, there's a lot of fear surrounding carbs, and people would rather just go without. Why are people so scared of this fundamental nutrient? That's wrong. It's wrong to be scared of bread, it's wrong to be scared of rice. You need to remove this concept from your head – that bread, roti or rice is bad for you.

Carbs are energy. Huge chunks of your diet *have* to be made up of carb calories. They not only enhance your mood, but also perform life-giving functions like aiding the absorption of calcium and phosphorus. And the kicker? Carbohydrates are integral to the normal metabolism of fats.

SIMPLE CARBS

There are two types of carbohydrates: simple and complex. Simple carbohydrates are basically sugars and they have almost no nutritional value. These are your chocolates, sugary drinks, sweets and cakes. They are 'simple' carbohydrates because your body doesn't have to do much to break them down. They pass through your body without nourishing it. You eat, you feel the sugar high and then, after a short interval, you crash. Not only do these bursts of energy wreak havoc with your system, simple carbs wind up making you feeling hungry, so you eat more, which in turn sabotages your efforts to lose weight.

COMPLEX CARBS

On the other hand, complex carbohydrates release energy into the body far more slowly. You feel fuller, more satisfied, and you don't have sudden spikes and crashes. You have a stable source of energy, which doubles up as a source of nourishment. Potatoes, barley, yams, sweet potatoes, rice, corn, beans, wholewheat, vegetables and fruit are all excellent sources of complex carbs. Plus, they are a prime source of dietary fibre – both soluble and insoluble – so that you have enough roughage to ensure that your bowel movements are normal and regular.

Nutrition Facts	
Serving Size 1 bag 7 oz 198g (198 g)	
Amount Per Serving	
Calories 972	Calories from Fat 558
	% Daily Value*
Total Fat 64g	99%
Saturated Fat 16g	80%
Trans Fat	
Cholesterol 0mg	0%
Sodium 1485mg	62%
Total Carbohydrate 105g	35%
Dietary Fiber 9g	35%
Sugars	
Protein 15g	
Vitamin A 9% • Vitamin C	112%
Calcium 10% • Iron	21%

And don't worry, carbs don't change their properties depending on the time you eat them. This whole no-carbs-at-night idea is sheer fallacy. It doesn't matter when you eat them. You need to reduce the overall quantity of food you eat towards the night, and try not to have heavy meals in the evening. But this is only because your level of activity is winding down; it has nothing to do with carbs. How can you be afraid of a nutrient that gives you energy, eases your bowel movements and takes care of your brain? Potatoes, bread, roti, rice are all part of my meal plans – even for diabetics. You just have to be careful about the *kind* of carbohydrate you put into your mouth.

DON'T DREAD THE BREAD

Whenever I work out meal plans for clients with diabetes, I spend more time convincing them to eat carbs than I do prescribing the diet! So what's fact, and what's fallacy?

If you have diabetes, the fact is that you need to be careful with your eating in order to regulate and manage your blood sugar. But you don't have to be afraid of carbs. Foods like carbs are higher in sugar, and need to be eaten carefully. The trick is to eat just enough for the body's sugar regulation.

Wanna eat rice or pasta? Boil it, throw out the water and don't have more than one bowl (30 grams when raw) in a day. Once you throw the rice's starchy water out, you are left with fibre – wonderful, glorious fibre that is good for you. If you're dying for some sweet fruit like chikoo, custard apple, mangoes and grapes, go ahead. Just make sure you don't eat more than 50 grams at a time (no more than 100 grams in the day, separated by at least two hours, and only as a standalone snack). Going nuts over potatoes? Divide 100 grams of potatoes over the day with 50 grams in your lunch or dinner and 50 grams in your evening poha or snack. Eating in smaller quantities ensures that your sugar levels don't spike and, instead, remain stable through the day.

Of course, you have to cut out sugary foods like cakes, mithai and the like but you need to manage your carbs just like you would manage your blood sugar. But do eat your potatoes, pasta and rice. You already have a long list of dos and don'ts as a diabetic. Please don't add fear to the list.

Label Guide: Look out for the following simple carbs on the nutritional label: high fructose corn syrup (HFCS), corn syrup, corn syrup solids, white sugar, raw sugar, brown sugar, malt syrup, pancake syrup, maple syrup, fructose sweetener, honey, liquid fructose, molasses, anhydrous dextrose and crystal dextrose or simply the word 'sugar'.[13] These are all various forms of high calorie sugars and you need to make an informed decision about how much of these you want to include in your life. For complex carbs, look for 'dietary fibre' on the label. You should not eat less than 6 grams of complex carbs per day.

---

[13] *American Dietary Guidelines*, 2010

GI FOODS

GI or Glycemic Index carbs are classified on the basis of their impact on your blood sugar. The higher the Glycemic Index of a particular food, the faster its breakdown in your body, the higher the spikes in your blood sugar. High GI foods leave you with an initial burst of energy which subsequently crashes, leaving you feeling slow and sluggish. For example, eating rice, which has a GI of 110, for lunch will make it harder for you to get back to work in the early afternoon. In comparison, low GI foods break down gradually, leading to a slower release of sugar in your body, helping you maintain energy levels through the day. While you don't have to obsessively follow this, it's a good-to-know for those who want to keep their energy levels stable and crucial for diabetics managing their sugars.

High GI: 70 and above
Medium GI: 56–69
Low GI: 55 and under

Food	*GI*
Low-fat yogurt	14
Asparagus	15
Broccoli	15
Cherries	22
Kidney beans (Rajma)	27
Low-fat milk	33
Apples	38
Carrots	39
Spaghetti	41
Apple juice	41
Grapes	46
Oatmeal	49
Whole grain bread	50
Yams	51
Orange juice	52
Sweet potato	54

Brown rice	55
Bananas	55
Popcorn	55
Potato chips	56
Cheese pizza	60
Ice-cream	61
Pineapple	66
White bread	75
French fries	75
Doughnuts	76
Waffles	76
Cornflakes	83
Baked potatoes	85
Dates	103
White rice	110

Source: Daniel G. Amen, *Change Your Brain, Change Your Body,* Harmony Books, 2010

Vitamins and Minerals

Don't forget your vitamins! One of the two micronutrients, vitamins don't have any calorific effect on your body, so they won't impact your weight loss efforts in either direction. But they are the helpers, without which crucial metabolic processes would not be possible. They are also different from the other four nutrients in that they are not produced by the body and have to be provided by an external source such as food or a pill (the exceptions are vitamins D and K which are produced by the body). Vitamins are only needed in small quantities, but they are needed.

YOU DON'T NEED MILK TO MAKE MILK

If you're a new mother and you think drinking lots of milk helps you produce good quality milk, this is for you: you don't need milk to make milk. What you eat in general contributes to the functioning of your mammary glands and allows you to breastfeed your baby.

To make milk, you need protein, sugar and water. So whether you eat spinach, eggs, meat, nuts or anything else, they are all broken down inside your body. Your body extracts what it needs from the food you eat to make milk. If you see a correlation between drinking and making milk, it is only because of the lactose and protein in milk. It's not the milk itself that makes milk.

There are three ways to produce good, nutrient-rich milk. First, you need to have a diet rich in protein (pulses and sprouts, paneer, milk, meat and dahi) which will enhance both milk production and quality. Second, you need to drink enough water. Water is a crucial element of lactation; it's so important that nursing mothers need to drink two glasses of water with every feed (the less water they drink, the less their flow of milk). And finally, small snacks between main meals help produce enough calories for you to produce good quality milk for your baby.

While the need for vitamins cannot be overemphasized, they are in danger of being over-administered. And because the perception is that vitamins are 'harmless', this is a common problem.

Many of my clients take a whole host of vitamins. In fact, many unknowingly duplicate the benefits that a pill or multivitamin gives them because they go to different healthcare practitioners or doctors, for example, a trichologist, a dermatologist and a general practitioner. Many people take separate antioxidants, separate vitamin E and C pills, separate cod liver oil pills and primrose oil pills, all at the same time. Some even take the same multivitamin under different brand names.

If you're treating yourself for deficiencies of vitamins A, D, E and K, remember that these are fat-soluble vitamins and need fat to absorb them. So when you overdose on these (and you don't need much of these to begin with), your body will not be able to expel

Nutrition Facts	
Serving Size 1 bag 7 oz 198g (198 g)	

Amount Per Serving	
Calories 972	Calories from Fat 558

	% Daily Value*
Total Fat 64g	99%
Saturated Fat 16g	80%
Trans Fat	
Cholesterol 0mg	0%
Sodium 1485mg	62%
Total Carbohydrate 105g	35%
Dietary Fiber 9g	35%
Sugars	
Protein 15g	

Vitamin A	9%	Vitamin C	112%
Calcium	10%	Iron	21%

this excess naturally. The excess consumption will be stored in your fat cells, leading to toxicity. Vitamins B and C have a pre-determined dosage as well, but these are water-soluble vitamins and the excess can be excreted out of your body.

MINERALS regulate many body functions including clotting of blood, contraction of muscles and control of water balance. Ninety per cent of the minerals that make up our bodies consist of chlorine and magnesium. The big daddies of this group of micronutrients are calcium and phosphorus (which help in bone building), iron (which is necessary for the formation of haemoglobin) as well as potassium and sodium (which help regulate blood pressure).

Water

This needs no label. Water is life itself. Our body is composed of anywhere between 55 to 78 per cent of it. About two-thirds of our body is water – the muscles are 75 per cent water, the brain is 90 per cent water, our bones are 22 per cent water and blood is 83 per cent water. Water is needed for respiration, circulation, temperature regulation, digestion, waste elimination, glandular secretion – practically all bodily functions. Water aids in the lubrication, insulation, protection and flexibility of muscles, ligaments and joints.

And yet we simply don't get enough.

If you really want to get on the express train to weight loss, you have to start tanking up on the H20. You need your mandatory 8 to 10 glasses a day, and this does not include tea, coffee and other fluids.

Glug down the following facts:

❏ Research shows that water increases the rate at which you burn calories. Berlin's Franz-Volhard Clinical Research Centre reported that after drinking 17 ounces of water, the metabolic rate of participants increased by 30 per cent.

❏ The liver produces bile so that we can digest the fat we consume. When we don't get enough water, it affects the production of bile, which affects our ability to digest fat.

❏ In our body, the hunger and thirst centres are very close to each other. When we don't drink enough water, dehydration often gets confused with hunger, and we eat when what we are actually feeling is acute thirst.

❏ When you drink enough water, you feel fuller. Portion control and your new weight loss lifestyle become so much easier.

❏ The greater the amount of physical activity you do, the more water you need to drink to replenish what you have lost through sweat.

❏ In many cases, water retention is not because you drink too much water, it's because you don't get enough.

The best part about this zero-calorie wonder is that it's free, readily available and you can get your fill wherever you are. Carry a bottle with you and guzzle-as-you-go, and you'll be surprised at how much faster those kilos drop.

RETAINING WATER?
DRINK MORE TO LOSE MORE

Ever wondered why you feel bloated and puffy, as though you have gained inches overnight? Do you find that your rings are suddenly too tight for your fingers? Or that just gently pressing your skin leaves dents? And even your shoes don't seem to fit? These could be symptoms of oedema or water retention.

Most of us do retain water, but within normal parameters. Women are more prone to water retention because it is a symptom of Premenstrual Syndrome (PMS). However, water retention could also be a symptom of kidney disease or heart, liver or thyroid malfunction, so if you feel that the bloating is not normal, do get yourself checked.

How to deal with excess retention of water:

❏ *Drink more to lose more.* To significantly reduce the amount of water being retained by your body, drink *more* water. It's a bit of a contradiction, but think about it – the more water you drink, the more your body will flush out. This is one of the most effective ways to combat water retention. Ten or twelve glasses a day ought to do the trick.

❏ *Eat smart to lose more.* Diets low in sodium (read: no table salt, pickle, papad, cheese, butter or processed food) and high in potassium (bananas, peaches, plums, musk melons, raisins) help maintain correct electrolyte balance within the body, preventing puffiness. Diuretic fruits like cranberries, vitamin C-rich oranges, limes and other citrus fruits, along with diuretic vegetables like cucumber, lettuce, celery, tomatoes, cabbage, carrots and peppers help maintain the correct osmolarity within your cells, preventing them from retaining excess water. Some studies show that vitamin B6 tablets (pyridoxine) and primrose oil capsules have the same benefits.

❏ *Cut back to lose more.* Additionally, avoiding alcohol and caffeinated beverages, anti-inflammatory drugs and oral contraceptives also help reduce water retention in the body.

❏ *Move more to lose more.* Get out and get moving – exercise works wonders! Also, avoid standing for long periods, don't wear very tight clothing and keep your legs raised as and when you can to avoid discomfort.

EAT!

Making a Fist

If the Five Fingers of Weight Loss were about the essentials of smart eating, a Fist consists of carefully thought out meal plans, customized to your BMR. I combine the best of macronutrients and micronutrients to provide you with the healthiest ways to eat your way to weight loss. These have been put together after years of administering similar meal plans to my clients who have reached their respective goal weights. Turn the page to turn over a new leaf.

STEP ONE | CALCULATE YOUR BMR

While I've already given you the formula for calculating your BMR, I am reproducing it here for ease of reference. Find out what your BMR is now!

Women's BMR	Men's BMR
655	66
+ (9.6 × your weight in kilos)	**+** (13.7 × your weight in kilos)
+ (1.8 × your height in cm)	**+** (5 × your height in cm)
− (4.7 × your age in years)	**−** (6.8 × your age in years)
= _____ calories per day	**=** _____ calories per day

STEP TWO | CUT 100 CALORIES FROM YOUR BMR

For example, if your BMR is 1580, choose a meal plan that is 100 calories lower, i.e., choose from the 1400 to 1600 calorie meal plans.

STEP THREE | PICK THE MEAL PLAN RANGE YOU FALL INTO

Choose from the following:

1200–1400 calories
1400–1600 calories
1600–1800 calories
1800–2000 calories
2000–2200 calories

STEP FOUR | EAT EVERY TWO HOURS

Yup, that's the rule. But don't go mad setting a timer. Fifteen or twenty minutes give or take will do.

STEP FIVE | EAT FOUR MEALS AND FOUR FILLERS

Besides outlining the main meals in each calorie range, I have also provided you with a list of fillers or snacks to eat between meals.

STEP SIX | DRINK PLENTY OF WATER THROUGH THE DAY
Tank up on at least 8 to 10 glasses of water every day.

STEP SEVEN | EXERCISE
While I usually recommend that you walk for an hour daily, any cardio activity will do. You can run, jog, cycle, get on the stepper, use the cross-trainer or even exercise using a combination of any of the above, but you have to do it for 60 minutes.

HOW TO MAKE A DELISH
VEGGIE JUICE

A glass of vegetable juice is a MUST MUST MUST on my programme, and it's as important to drink this every day as it is to eat every two hours. Unlike fruit juices, which spike your sugar levels, vegetable juices provide a concentrated burst of glorious vitamins and antioxidants. You can make it in minutes with veggies you find in your house. Small effort, huge reward.

❏ Wash all vegetables thoroughly. A final rinse with potassium permanganate is also recommended.
❏ Choose a minimum of 3 different vegetables (preferably of 3 different colours so that you get a host of vitamins and minerals) Peel and cut vegetables and put in a mixer (not in a juicer, as juicers require more vegetables).
❏ Add water – the juice should be a combination of water and vegetables in about the same proportion.
❏ Blend and strain the juice into a glass.
❏ Take 50 per cent of the roughage (pulp that you have taken out) and put it back into the glass.
❏ Add some flavouring or seasoning if you like (rock salt, pepper, fresh ginger).
❏ Drink up immediately!

The Eat Sheet

To get a 10 out of 10 on your weight loss, do make note of the following 10 steps before you start your meal plans.

1. Eat within the first hour of rising.
2. Drink 8 to 12 glasses of water a day.
3. Each meal plan has four main meals (breakfast, lunch, evening snack and dinner).
4. Anything else you eat in between has to be taken from the Filler List at the end this chapter. Please choose only one filler at a time between your main meals. Your evening snack should be a combination of filler items (as per your meal plan).
5. Of the fillers you need to have between meals, vegetable juice must be one of them (certain vegetable combinations may not be allowed depending upon individual blood and urine analysis. Please check this with your doctor.).
6. No sugar, honey, artificial sweeteners, gur, nuts, dry fruits, fried food, cheese or dessert are allowed in this phase of weight loss.
7. Try to make breakfast with no oil. Also, you won't be able to consume any fat apart from oil. So your meal plans cannot include ghee, khoa or butter.
8. You can substitute one katori dal with 2 pieces of chicken (leg and thigh) or 2 palm-sized pieces of fish.
9. All fruits except bananas allowed. 1 serving = 100 grams. However, fruit juices are not allowed.
10. Peas and potatoes should be no more than 100 grams per day. Understand your portions

> 1 bowl = holds 180ml of water
> 1 roti = a 5.5 inch diameter palm-size thin roti (This is just an approximation. Don't go nuts.)

The nutritional advice given here does not account for any pre-existing conditions like diabetes or PCOS. Please get this plan approved by your doctor before embarking on the programme.

Meal Plans

1200 TO 1400 CALORIES

❏ This is an estimation of a 1200 to 1400 calorie meal plan.

❏ You have to eat 4 main meals (breakfast, lunch, evening snack, dinner) and 4 fillers.

❏ Added oil should not exceed 2 to 3 teaspoons per day. This is a mandate for the successful execution of the programme.

BREAKFAST

OPTION 1	OPTION 2	OPTION 3	OPTION 4
1 bowl upma/ poha with ½ bowl vegetables 1 fruit	1 bowl cornflakes 1 cup skimmed milk 1 fruit	1 glass veggie juice 1 fruit 2 egg whites 1 slice bread	1 stuffed roti 1 bowl curd 1 fruit

LUNCH AND DINNER

Pick any two options – one for lunch and one for dinner

OPTION 1	OPTION 2	OPTION 3	OPTION 4	OPTION 5
2 roti 1 bowl vegetables ½ bowl dal	1 roti ½ bowl steamed rice 1 bowl vegetables ½ bowl dal	1 bowl steamed rice 1 bowl vegetables ½ bowl dal	1 small roti 1 slice bread 1 bowl vegetables ½ bowl dal	2 slices bread ½ bowl vegetable soup ½ bowl sprouts salad 1 vegetable cutlet

EVENING SNACK

Your evening snack should be a combination of any 2 filler items

ARTIFICIAL SWEETENERS:
THE BITTER TRUTH

They come in sachets, in powder form or in small tablets but ultimately, when you are aware of the side effects of artificial sweeteners, it is a bitter pill to swallow. Here are some lesser known facts about sugar substitutes: Aspartame (the primary sweetening ingredient in Equal, NutraSweet, Sugar Free Gold; also present in Diet Coke, Diet Pepsi to name a few) was rejected by FDA a record *eight* times before it was finally approved for unrestricted use in 1996. Aspartame has been linked with memory loss, migraines, nerve-cell damage, reproductive disorders, brain lesions, mental confusion, joint pains, bloating, Alzheimer's, nervous system disorders, food cravings, hair loss. Oh, and I forgot one – weight gain. And these are just a few of the 92 FDA-listed official side effects of this sweetener.

Sucralose (Splenda, Sugar Free, Natura) has been touted as a 'safe' alternative as it is 'made from sugar'. I don't know how safe it is if it has been linked with diarrhoea, organ, genetic, reproductive and immune system damage, swelling of the kidneys and liver, and decrease in foetal body weight. Saccharine (Sweet and Low) is a compound of coal and tar.

For every study ruling out the negative effects of sweeteners, there is one that links them with a new disease. The fact of the matter is that the debate still rages on, and when in doubt, eliminate. If you can't completely banish, drastically cut down your intake. There are safer and easier alternatives to losing weight.

Stevia (sold under the brand name Dr Sugar in India) is one such alternative. This completely natural, herbal, calorie-free sweetener is a far healthier alternative to chemical-based sweeteners, and has weight loss benefits. It is also associated with lowering blood pressure and improving digestion.*

* Ron Freedman and Kim Barnouin, *Skinny Bitch*, Running Press, 2005

1400 TO 1600 CALORIES

❏ This is an estimation of a 1400 to 1600 calorie meal plan.

❏ You have to eat 4 main meals and 4 fillers.

❏ Added oil should not exceed 2 to 3 teaspoons per day.

BREAKFAST

OPTION 1	OPTION 2	OPTION 3	OPTION 4
1 bowl upma/ poha with ½ bowl vegetables 1 glass veggie juice 1 fruit	½ bowl cornflakes 1 cup skimmed milk 1 fruit 1 vegetable sandwich	1 glass veggie juice 1 fruit 2 egg whites 2 slices bread	2 stuffed roti 1 bowl curd 1 fruit

LUNCH AND DINNER

Pick any two – one for lunch and one for dinner

OPTION 1	OPTION 2	OPTION 3	OPTION 4
3 roti 1 bowl vegetables 1 bowl dal or ½ bowl dal + 1 cup curd	2 roti ½ bowl steamed rice 1 bowl vegetables 1 bowl dal	1 roti 1 bowl steamed rice 1 bowl vegetables 1 bowl dal ½ bowl curd	3 slices bread ½ bowl vegetable soup 1 bowl sprouts salad 1 vegetable cutlet

EVENING SNACK

Your evening snack should be a combination of 2 filler items

NO FRUIT AFTER SUNSET

Why would anyone ever tell you not to have a healthy, nutritive fruit post sunset? This has no scientific basis. Please ignore this bit of 'advice'. All you need to remember is that if you are eating fruit at night it needs to be eaten one or two hours after your main meal and not with it or immediately after it (as it otherwise spikes your sugars and gets stored as fat) and a minimum one hour before bedtime (because again, it will spike your sugars and get stored as fat).

1600 TO 1800 CALORIES

❏ This is an estimation of a 1600-1800 calorie meal plan.

❏ You have to eat 4 main meals and 4 fillers.

❏ Added oil should not exceed 2 to 4 teaspoons per day.

BREAKFAST

OPTION 1	OPTION 2	OPTION 3	OPTION 4
1 bowl upma/ poha with ½ bowl vegetables 1 glass veggie juice 1 fruit	½ bowl cornflakes 1 cup skimmed milk 1 fruit 1 vegetable sandwich	1 glass veggie juice 1 fruit 2 egg whites 2 slices bread	2 stuffed roti 1 bowl curd 1 fruit

LUNCH AND DINNER

Pick any two – one for lunch and one for dinner

OPTION 1	OPTION 2	OPTION 3	OPTION 4
4 roti 1 bowl vegetables 1 bowl dal	3 roti ½ bowl steamed rice 1 bowl vegetable 1 bowl dal	2 roti 1 bowl steamed rice 1 bowl vegetables 1 bowl dal	3 slices bread 1 roti ½ bowl vegetable soup 1 bowl sprouts salad 1 vegetable cutlet

EVENING SNACK

Your evening snack should be a combination of 2 filler items

ALCOHOL AND WEIGHT LOSS? A FRUITLESS COCKTAIL

This is not just the wine talking. At a massive 7 calories per gram, alcohol is one of the most fattening things you can ingest. Carbs and proteins stack up at 4 calories per gram, which means that alcohol has *more* calorific content than bread, rice, pasta or potatoes. Yikes!

And it's not just its calorie count. As you now know, our body derives energy from different sources of food like carbs, protein and fat. When alcohol enters our system, it gets converted into something called acetate. Acetate is a primary source of fuel which our body burns first. So, instead of burning the cheese that we've just eaten or the pasta that we've just savoured, our body will first burn the wine or beer or vodka we have consumed. Acetate pushes fat burning to the back of the queue and replaces fat as a source of fuel. This puts the brakes on the process of fat loss.

Alcohol doesn't just restrict fat loss. It also stimulates your appetite levels for up to 24 hours after you've finished drinking. This is why you can't seem to resist bar food, midnight snacks and binge-eating after that night out.

While there are studies that suggest that a glass of red wine every day helps prevent heart disease and lowers cholesterol, oats, bran, nuts, fresh fruits and vegetables perform the same function and don't have any side effects.

A single shot of liquor (1.5 ounces) can contain anything between 115 and 200 calories. In comparison, a 4-ounce glass of wine contains between 62 and 160 calories. Mixed drinks are where the calories really add up, ranging from approximately 280 calories for a gin and tonic to over 800 calories for some of the frozen, creamy drinks. One beer every night adds up to 1036 additional calories per week, or 6 to 7 kilos to your stomach every year! No wonder it's called a beer belly.

How to drink smart:

❏ Convert your wine into a spritzer (a soda-diluted long drink) – it has fewer calories.

❏ Alternate alcoholic drinks with low-calorie non-alcoholic drinks or water. For instance, drink one glass of water or nimbu paani for every glass of white wine.

❏ Ask for low-calorie mixers where possible. Avoid pre-mixed ready alcoholic beverages as these contain lots of sugar.

❏ Plan your alcohol into your daily calorie quota so that you can enjoy a glass or two. If you know you will be drinking during the weekend, try to save some calories each day in advance, so you can eat normally before you go out.

❏ Do not be tempted to skip meals for drinks, as alcohol will not satisfy your hunger. And, as alcohol stimulates appetite, eating a proper meal before you go out will line your stomach and slow the rate at which alcohol is absorbed by your bloodstream, keeping you in control of how much you eat and drink.

1800 TO 2000 CALORIES

❏ This is an estimation of an 1800 to 2000 calorie meal plan.

❏ You have to eat 4 main meals and 8 fillers.

❏ Added oil should not exceed 2 to 4 teaspoons per day.

BREAKFAST

OPTION 1	OPTION 2	OPTION 3	OPTION 4
1 bowl upma/ poha with ½ bowl vegetables 1 glass veggie juice 1 fruit	½ bowl cornflakes 1 cup skimmed milk 1 fruit 1 vegetable sandwich	1 glass veggie juice 1 fruit 2 egg whites 2 slices bread	2 stuffed roti 1 bowl curd 1 fruit

LUNCH AND DINNER

Pick any two – one for lunch and one for dinner

OPTION 1	OPTION 2	OPTION 3	OPTION 4
4 roti 1 bowl vegetables 1 bowl dal	3 roti ½ bowl steamed rice 1 bowl vegetables 1 bowl dal	2 roti 1 bowl steamed rice 1 bowl vegetables 1 bowl dal	3 slices bread 1 roti ½ bowl vegetable soup 1 bowl sprouts salad 1 vegetable cutlet

EVENING SNACK

Your evening snack should be a combination of 2 filler items

DRINKING WITHOUT THINKING

It's the U-Turn many don't even know they have taken. Many of my clients who have worked hard to *eat* their way to weight loss unknowingly *drink* their way back to weight gain. Whether it's a cola, smoothie, cocktail or fruit lassi, liquid calories can derail your weight loss programme faster than anything else. If you're in the weight loss phase, please watch out for all sugary drinks; I'll show you how to re-integrate these back into your system in the maintenance phase.

But what's the deal with fruit juices? Aren't they supposed to be healthy? Actually, no. Not even freshly squeezed juice without sugar. When you drink any liquid, it quickly enters your bloodstream and the active nutrients are absorbed first. The most active nutrient in fruit juice is fructose. Fructose gets speedily absorbed in your bloodstream and raises – and subsequently slashes – your blood sugar levels, making you feel tired and sluggish (not to mention that it's a strict no-no for diabetics). Since your body can't utilize that much sugar at one time, it gets stored as fat. Packed or tinned fruit juices are the worst. They have high levels of sugar and their nutritive value has been all but stripped, and that goes for the fortified ones as well. You might as well boil sugar and swallow it.

But the same does not hold true in the case of vegetable juice. A glass of vegetable juice is a must on my programme and I tell all my clients to drink it, no matter what. In the case of vegetable juice, the active nutrients are vitamins and minerals. So when you drink this juice, vitamins and minerals are absorbed faster by your body and you can see the positive effects on your skin and in your energy levels.

Eat fruit as opposed to drinking it. When you eat fruit, your sugar levels are beautifully maintained *and* you get all the fibre and goodness which you won't get in its liquid form. Think before you drink – it can help your weight loss efforts and your health.

2000 TO 2200 CALORIES

❏ This is an estimation of a 2000 to 2200 calorie meal plan.
❏ You have to eat 4 main meals and 8 fillers.
❏ Added oil should not exceed 2 to 4 teaspoons per day.

BREAKFAST

OPTION 1	OPTION 2	OPTION 3	OPTION 4
2 bowl upma/ poha with 1 bowl vegetables 1 glass veggie juice 1 fruit	1 bowl cornflakes 1 cup skimmed milk 1 fruit 1 vegetable sandwich	1 glass veggie juice 1 fruit 3 egg whites 3 slices bread	3 stuffed roti 1 bowl curd 1 fruit

LUNCH AND DINNER

Pick any two – one for lunch and one for dinner

OPTION 1	OPTION 2	OPTION 3	OPTION 4
4 roti 1 bowl vegetables 1 ½ bowls dal	3 roti ½ bowl steamed rice 1 ½ bowls dal 1 bowl vegetables	1 bowl steamed rice 2 roti 1 bowl vegetables 1 ½ bowls dal	3 slices bread 1 roti ½ bowl vegetable soup 1 bowl sprouts salad 1 vegetable cutlet 1 cup curd

EVENING SNACK

Your evening snack should be a combination of 4 filler items

DON'T GET BROWNED OFF

It's a myth that refined foods – white rice, pasta, flour, bread – lead to weight gain. While it is true that refined foods are stripped of their minerals (the process of refining involves removing the bran and the husk), they are neither more nor less fattening than their unrefined avatars. Do remember that most cereals have miniscule amounts of the micronutrient to begin with, i.e., 10 rotis contain the same amount of minerals as a slice of apple.

The main disadvantage of refined foods is that they don't take much time to digest, and raise your blood sugar levels faster. Therefore, the only thing we need to remember when we eat these foods is to keep track of the amount eaten at a particular time. Thus, in my meal plans, I never recommend you eat more than two biscuits at a time. Bread slices usually are never eaten more than one or two at a time, rice and pasta are never eaten more than a bowl at a time. As long as you remember to restrict the quantity, your blood sugar levels will be stable, allowing you to do more with your day.

QUINOA

Referred to by the ancient Incas as 'chisaya mama' or the 'mother of all grains', quinoa has been in existence for hundreds of years and its edible seeds have recently made their way back to our plates. Packed with goodness and health, quinoa looks like couscous when boiled and can be used in place of rice (the quantities won't change). It can also be used to make upma, poha or dalia. Roast it, grind it and make quinoa flour out of it to make nutritious rotis. It's a beautiful 100 per cent reference protein that contain all nine essential amino acids, including an abundance of lysine, which no other cereal has. Bon appetit!

Fillers

1. 2 biscuits (Marie/ KrackJack/ Glucose/ cream crackers/ Monaco)
2. 1 medium-sized diet khakra
3. 1 medium-sized idli
4. ½ medium-sized sada dosa
5. 17 grapes
6. 6 to 8 strawberries
7. 2 to 3 plums
8. 18 to 20 cherries
9. 4 medium slices pineapple (diameter of the slice is approximately 3 inches)
10. 1 medium-sized orange/ apple/ pear
11. 6 to 7 lychees
12. 1 bowl watermelon/ muskmelon/ papaya
13. 1 bowl skimmed-milk curd
14. 1 bowl kurmura (puffed rice)
15. ½ bowl sprouts salad
16. Small fistful of channa and 1 glass chhaas
17. 2 boiled egg whites and 1 cracker
18. Vegetable juice
19. ½ bowl vegetable poha
20. Open sandwich with vegetable toppings
21. Chicken and peppers on bread
22. ½ bowl upma with beans and carrots
23. ½ bowl roasted poha chivda with some chana
24. 2 tbsp cornflakes with skimmed milk
25. ½ bowl hakka noodles with veggies
26. ½ bowl pasta in red sauce with mushrooms
27. ½ bowl spaghetti with spinach
28. 1 bowl popcorn without butter
29. Cornflakes bhel (2tbsp corn/ wheat flakes + 2tbsp chopped vegetables)
30. 1tbsp hummus and 1 cracker

Get Moving to Get Losing

When I was growing up, there was an irritating boy who always used to annoy me by hitting me on the arm and then running away. We used to spend the better part of an hour chasing each other to see who hit whom next, and we kept playing till we couldn't run any more. Tired – and friends again – we'd share the day's 'loot' – a seashell, a rusted key, a bicycle chain, whatever we found fascinating or shiny. Or both.

I didn't know it then but I was getting the workout of my life.

Forget everything you have seen in weight loss ads, gym commercials or celebrity endorsements. Exercise is NOT a chore. You are supposed to have a whale of a time. Remember when you were a child? You ran, you played, you jumped. You impressed your friends with your dance steps, or made it a mission to beat each other at badminton, tennis, football or running on the beach. You made teams – boys versus girls or 10th standard versus 12th standard. You played chor-police, dabba, pakram-pakri. And you burned loads of calories the entire time.

To lose a good amount of weight, what you need is to boost your heartbeat and sweat it out for an hour every day or at least 4 or 5 times a week. What you *don't* need to do is to dread the hour of exercise you've planned for yourself. If it's something you hate, it only means you haven't yet found something you love.

And it's not just about losing weight. I believe exercising is like paying for silver and getting diamonds in return. Just getting out there, getting your heart pumping and your blood flowing and working out for a sexy, new you have been associated with reducing the risks of cardiovascular disease, Type II diabetes, blood pressure and developing healthy bones, muscles and joints. Psychological benefits include improved self-esteem and reduced feelings of anxiety and depression. No amount of watchful eating can compensate for these wonderful benefits.

I find that that most of my clients reach their goal weight by doing the simplest of all activities – brisk walking. It's the most basic way to get in shape. But exercise has many avatars. You can get a fantastic workout on the badminton court, or shed kilos by thrashing your college buddies at tennis or squash. You can swim, take spinning, zumba or aerobics classes. There are even classes for pole dancing. You can work out alone or get a buddy to train with you. You may not find the answer in the four mirrored corners of your neighbourhood gym. Or you just might. And mix it up – you don't need to be consistent with the *type* of exercise you do – you can run one day, go spinning another. All you need to do is be consistent with exercise itself.

Boosting activity levels is also an effective way to drop those kilos. This phenomenon is called NEAT (Non-exercise Activity Thermogenesis) and in a nutshell, it means that any level of non-exercise related activity (just moving around and going about your day) has a direct relationship with the management of obesity.[14] The more you move, the more you lose. It's scientific fact.

If you're at work, walk when you're talking on the phone, take the stairs, walk smaller distances. Don't send your assistant to pass a message to your colleague. Get out of your cubicle and stretch

---

[14] Shashank Joshi, *Primer of Obesity*

your legs. If you're at home, don't send your maid out to buy things for the house. Take your shopping bag and go. You get the idea. If you don't have an exclusive hour to set aside for exercise and are strapped for time, strap on a pedometer instead. A pedometer is a device which counts the number of steps you take in a day. Ten thousand steps a day is enough to get you some good weight loss and you'd be surprised at how easy it is to reach this target.

Please remember that any and all activity is being silently added up by your body. And when the weight starts coming off, you will realize that your body rewards you for every little thing you do.

'If I Exercise, I Can Eat What I Want'

So many clients come in with the misconception that they can 'eat what they want so long as they're working out'. I wish you could, but unfortunately it doesn't work that way. I mean, maybe you could if you were training for the Olympics or something like that – working out then becomes your job. But most of us have sedentary professions coupled with sedentary lifestyles. Exercise is a way to complement our efforts, but it is not – and should never be taken as – a standalone solution to weight loss.

It's like this. If you eat a 1000-calorie burger, it will take about two hours jogging to work it off. Isn't it just easier not to eat the burger? Exercise will boost your weight loss and tone your body and is an irreplaceable part of my programme. But there is a fixed amount of calories it can burn. Because there is only a fixed amount of time you can devote to it.

SIDDHARTH MALLYA'S CHECKLIST FOR GETTING FIT

- ❑ Did you set some time aside for exercise today? Make an effort to schedule exercise once a day or at least 4 to 5 times a week for some physical activity be it walking, swimming, cycling or weight lifting.

- ❑ Are you okay with not always having a gym or a class to exercise in? There's this perception that if you don't have a gym, you can't exercise. That's not true. You can exercise anywhere you are because all you have to do is keep yourself active. When I was in the US recently, I did Pilates in my hotel room.

- ❑ Do you look forward to your exercise routine? You MUST make exercise enjoyable. And when you start seeing results, you'll enjoy it even more!

- ❑ Are you increasing your level of physical activity? Keep doing something – if there's a choice between a lift or a flight of stairs, take the stairs. In the airports, don't stand on the moving walkways, walk on them.

- ❑ Do you want to spend more time with yourself? Exercise is your time with yourself – no email, no mobile, nothing. It's your time to focus on YOU.

MY IDEAL WEEKLY EXERCISE EQUATION

   cardio
 + light weight training (to increase BMR)
 + move around more
 = a hot, toned body

This is just a recommendation of how to exercise during the week – you can go to a dance class once a week, walk twice a week, lift weights twice a week and just get more active on a day-to-day basis. It's advisable to start slow, especially if you haven't been working out in a while. You can consult your doctor but listen to your body: it will tell you when to stop and when to keep going.

Well, what are you waiting for?

Get moving to get losing.

SMALL CHANGE, BIG LOSE

Making these small changes can make you lose by the kilo!

1. **Milk your weight loss.** Get the most out of your weight loss efforts by replacing regular milk with non-fat or 2 per cent milk (98 per cent fat free). Even if you drink just two cups of tea a day, this simple switch can result in weight loss of 2.7 kilos a year or more.

2. **Go easy on the greasy.**
   ❏ By simply eliminating sev and papdi from your bhel, you can lose up to 2 kilos per year (if you eat bhel once or twice a week).
   ❏ Make your popcorn without butter or oil and save a cool 100 calories every time!
   ❏ Chapati without ghee can save you a massive 6.4 kilos a year, assuming you eat 3 rotis a day; many of you eat more!
   ❏ Chapatis without ghee can save you loads of saturated fats, keeping your bad cholesterol under control. Chapatis without ghee eliminate 3558 mg of cholesterol from your diet per year. Similarly, eliminating butter from bread or toast saves you 8030 mg of cholesterol per year.
   ❏ Replace butter with dhaniya chutney in your sandwich. If you love sandwiches and eat them regularly (four times a week or more), this simple switch makes you 2.4 kilos lighter each year!

3. **Dethrone the cone.** Ice-cream cones are made from sugar and flour. Ice-cream in a cup saves you 100 calories every time!

4. **Think before you drink.** Switch your glass of white wine with a white wine spritzer (one-third wine, two-third soda). And get ready to lose 1 or 2 kilos a year!

5. **Dress it down.** Dress your salads with lime, vinaigrette and balsamic vinegar and ditch Thousand Island, mayo and Caesar dressings. This little change will give you a big lose of up to 400 calories every time. If you eat salads twice a week, that's weight loss of over 4 kilos a year!

6. **Sharing is losing.** The more you share your dessert, the fewer calories you have to burn off!

7. **Sweeten your life.** Don't put sugar in your tea. If you put 2 teaspoons of sugar in each cup and have two cups of tea a day, your pancreas will secrete 5.2 units of insulin more every day. By not adding sugar, you save 1898 units of insulin per year, increasing the life of your pancreas and preventing the onset of Type II diabetes. It'll only take a few weeks for your taste buds to adjust.

8. **Eat fruit, don't drink it.** Fruit juice has a high Glycemic Index (GI) which spikes your blood sugar and gets stored as fat.

9. **Don't say cheese.** Pizza without cheese tastes just as delicious and saves you tons of calories every year. For every two slices you eat without cheese, you save yourself from burning 200 excess calories each time. If you eat pizza twice a week, you save almost 2.7 kilos a year just by removing the cheese.

10. **Open your sandwich.** Close the door to weight gain. Open sandwiches – using just one bread slice and not two – save you approximately 100 calories every time. If you're someone who eats sandwiches regularly (four times a week or more), you can save 2.7 kilos a year by taking this one simple step!

11. **Mellow the yellow.** Just eliminating the egg yolk from your daily egg can save you 2.9 kilos a year!

12. **Better to be safe than khari.** All you chai-time snackers, eliminate eating khari (flaky pastry biscuit) biscuits with your daily tea. One small khari has 100 calories. This simple move saves you 4.7 kilos a year!

13. **Hang weight gain.** One tablespoon of hung curd dressing versus regular mayo saves you a kilo a year!

14. **Waste makes waist.** Listen to this! Eating leftovers from your child's or spouse's plate or snacking while cooking leads you to pile on the kilos without even realizing it. Letting unfinished food go to waste or storing it in the fridge for the next meal can help you lose up to 4.7 kilos a year! Beat that!

15. **Sit down to scale down.** Sit and eat. When you sit, the shape of the stomach ensures that you eat less. When you're standing, your stomach is flattened out, and you need more food to feel full.

In Black and White
The Diary of a Dieter

'I have to write everything I eat? Everything? Every day?'
Twenty-three-year-old Neha had PCOS, 20 kilos to lose, and she seemed to be in the right frame of mind to start her weight loss programme. She was ready to eat food cooked in less oil, kill the junk food and go easy on the sugary stuff. From three times a day, she was prepared to eat every two hours. She was also all set to exercise five times a week – there was a zumba class she wanted to try out. She was willing to make all these changes in her life but she was not ready to maintain a food diary.

Let me answer some of the questions she asked me, so that you can understand why this is one of the most important aspects of your new nutritional programme. And why, if you don't do it, you might as well give up your weight loss efforts entirely.

Why? What's the point?'
Food diaries are an accurate record of exactly what you've been eating from the moment you wake up to the moment you fall asleep. You need to write down every single thing you eat, whether it's a piece of fruit or what you ate at dinner. Diaries make you accountable, and work both as conscience and guide. If you are

not losing weight at the pace you want to, just look into your food diary and the answers will be there in black-and-white.

Every single thing you eat has an impact on your weight – from the extra cookie you gobbled up to the teaspoon of ghee you added to your roti. These two food items already add about 150 calories, if not more. By not recording what you are eating, you will forget you ate these in the first place, and then wonder why you are not losing weight.

Food diaries also work very well for those who are intolerant towards or allergic to certain foods but are not aware of what's causing the problem. Writing down what you ate gives you a chance to figure out the reason behind a bout of nausea or constipation. Diaries also work for diabetics taking insulin dosage and who have to work to maintain stable sugars.

But I can keep track of what I eat, Pooja! I swear! I have a good memory.

Yes, Neha, you may have a good memory. But try and recall what you ate last Tuesday. Or why you weighed more on Monday morning. Chances are you will not remember what you ate, but you *will* remember feeling bloated or sluggish. And you will definitely remember that you didn't lose weight that week. All you are left with is the result without being able to identify the cause, which is not very motivating.

Which Is More Accurate?[15]

But if I start writing everything I'll get fed up!

On the contrary, writing a food diary will only help you stick to your plan. Not only will you be able to keep track of why you are both gaining and losing weight, you will also be confident that if

---

[15] Judith Beck, *The Beck DIET Solution*, Oxmoor House, 2008

8 a.m.	1 apple
9 a.m.	5 egg-white omelette with a slice of toast
11 a.m.	1 glass vegetable juice
1 p.m.	2 rotis +1 bowl dal + 1 bowl vegetables
3 p.m.	1 guava
5 p.m.	Dry bhel with tea
7 p.m.	1 cup low-fat dahi
8 p.m.	1 bowl rice with 2 pieces chicken and curry
10 p.m.	1 apple

OR

I managed not to have the pastry at dinner yesterday. By and large, I think I followed my meal plan properly. I don't remember what I ate at teatime but it should be all right.

you are eating correctly and exercising, you have done everything in your power to lose weight. The weight loss is inevitable.

'I don't have the time!'

Five minutes a day. That's all you need. Keep it in the loo with the pen handy or on your bedside table and fill it in before you sleep at night. Shove it into your office drawer or keep it in your car or your purse or your briefcase. You can fill it on the go.

'I can't carry a separate book around. It's painful.'

You don't have to carry a separate diary. Many of my clients write their food intake in their daily diaries – in which they write everything – and simply include the food they eat. School children write in their notebooks; every page is a 'day'.

You can also go digital. With iPads and laptops and cell-phones and PDAs, you can use any function that supports making a list, so long as you can keep a record. There are also loads of online diaries that are fun and interactive so you can even fill these during your Facebook break.

What do I need to write in it?

Every food diary must record the date, the time, the food eaten and the level of exercise or activity. Don't record your weight more than once a week, though. As I have told you already, weighing yourself daily is a pointless exercise. As weight fluctuates daily, it's either over-motivating (if you are weighing lighter one day) or de-motivating (if you are suddenly faced with a half kilo increase).

This diary format works well:

DAY/ DATE	
TIME	FOOD
	EXERCISE ___ MINUTES
	PEDOMETER ___ STEPS

Enjoy watching the kilos come off as you see the evidence of your new lifestyle both on the page and on your scale.

VIDYA BALAN'S CHECKLIST FOR
A GOOD NIGHT'S SLEEP

❏ Can you go to bed on time? Try to go to bed at about the same time every night. Routine is really important for regulating your body's sleep cycle.

❏ Could you avoid sleeping during the day? Sleeping during the day affects your nightly snooze. If you must nap, power nap for no more than 20 minutes.

❏ Have you stopped drinking coffee or tea after dinner? This one is self explanatory. Avoid, avoid, avoid caffeine!

❏ Can you stop eating heavy meals too close to your bedtime? Avoid eating heavy meals a few hours before sleeping. Digestion can keep you awake.

❏ Have you taken measures to reduce your stress? When there are too many thoughts running around in your head, it really interferes with your sleep.

Snooze to Lose

Taking Weight Loss Lying Down

By the time you reach this page, you've pretty much learned all there is to get your hot new body. Willpower, check. Food, check. Goal setting, check. So what's left? Well, this part of your weight loss programme involves no food diary, no meal plan and no exercise, yet it is crucial to losing it and keeping it off. This part requires you to get a pillow, snuggle under the covers, turn off the light and close your eyes.

Your body does not just run on food, water and air. Sleep is a vital component of its functioning. Without adequate sleep, you are setting yourself up for depression, irritability, reduced brain function, memory loss and obesity. Studies have repeatedly showed the glaring link between sleep deprivation and weight gain and still so many of us get far less than we need.

And here's why. There are two major factors in play when it comes to your appetite: leptin is your satiety hormone which tells your body that you have had enough to eat, and gives you that 'full' feeling. Ghrelin, on the other hand, is your hunger hormone and sends signals to your body that it needs food. There are studies that suggest that when you don't get adequate sleep, the level of leptin decreases and level of ghrelin increases.[16] In other

---

[16] 'Sleep Loss May Equal Weight Gain', http://www.usatoday.com/news/health/2004-12-06-sleep-weight-gain_x.htm accessed on 10/1/12

words, you don't feel full as fast you normally would, and you feel hungrier than you actually are.

Ironically, many of my clients cut back on their sleep to accommodate their new lifestyle. They see no problem in sleeping an hour less to squeeze in that gym time. Well, you'd be better off sleeping in.

If you're finding it a problem to get your 8 hours in bed, maybe the issue is with the way you are managing the 16 hours that you are awake. Are you taking on too much responsibility? Are you doing things you could pass on to someone else? Think about how your life is structured and what you need to downsize or just cut out. Ultimately, make space for sleep because it's hard to lose without clocking in the snooze.

FINISH

Speed Bumps

The Open Secret

I'm about to let you in on a little secret. Are you sitting down for this? Good, because I am about to reveal the ultimate truth about all of you who are embarking on your journey to losing weight. I'm about to tell you something no book on weight loss has ever told you. And the secret is this: You – yes, you, who have made a commitment to take charge of your weight and your life – are 100 per cent, genuinely, authentically HUMAN.

If you think your weight loss will progress smoothly, it won't. If you think that just by reading a book your body will immediately listen to your mind, it won't. If you've embarked on your new lifestyle and you feel overwhelmed and irritable, it is because you're human. You are reversing *years* of habits that have led to weight gain. Please don't expect more of yourself than you can give. You're human.

I can assure you – no, I can guarantee – that each and every one of you will encounter speed bumps on your way to the finish line – situations and environments that distract you from your goal. But the question is: will that speed bump have the power to pull you back to the starting line? Or will you face it head on, armed and ready to deal with it?

Your resistance to unhealthy foods will typically be lower at the start of your new lifestyle. You may not always be able to find reasons to stick to your diet, especially if the environment around you doesn't encourage it. I've enlisted the help of a nutrition and health psychologist to help you identify some common speed bumps and also learn to confront these situations, so that you are always prepared. If developing willpower is like learning to ride a bicycle, think of this chapter as providing a set of training wheels for the fittest ride of your life.

Situation

Social Event

What It Looks Like

From: true_fire78@hotmail.com
To: sloppysecs@gmail.com

Hey G, We're getting together Sat night. You HAVE to come. Nikhil was asking about you. Ma's making your favourite: rice kheer with badaam. And don't give me that diet nonsense. You're eating.

Love, me

What You're Thinking

I can't say no to aunty. What if she feels bad?

YOUR SPEED BUMP

Eating to Please

'I Can't Say No to Aunty'

Whether it's weddings, family functions or just dinner with friends, food is often tied to a host of social obligations. You can't not eat if someone's called you over – won't they be insulted? You can't not eat if your mother-in-law or sister-in-law or aunt made something special for you – won't that affect your relationship with them? And not eat at your mother's sister's friend's daughter's wedding? Won't your mother's sister's friend feel bad? Eating in these situations is all about making someone else happy.

When you eat to make other people happy, it often boils down to imagined disappointment. When we say 'it looks bad if I don't eat' or 'my mother-in-law made it so I have to eat', we often overestimate how hurt or upset the other person is going to be. We also overestimate how long that person is going to *stay* hurt. If you're eating to please, it's important to remember that while you may disappoint the other person, you will definitely disappoint yourself. Because, all the while, you are assuming how the other person is going to react.

I'm not saying you shouldn't try to make other people happy. I'm just saying that when it comes to your health, there are other ways to do so. Put yourself in the other person's shoes. If someone continually said 'no thanks', would you really hold a grudge against them? I'm sure you wouldn't. So why do you assume they will feel long-lasting hurt/ anger/ irritation if you refuse their offer? And if your host does stay mad at you for not eating, chances are they are holding a grudge against you for something besides food.

The goal of eating is to feel better, not guilty, afterwards. If you eat under pressure, not only will you not enjoy it but you will feel worse later – the weighing scale will judge you for it. Is it really worth sabotaging your attempts to lose weight for someone who doesn't appreciate your efforts to get healthy? What if you were a

Jain? No one would force you to eat chicken or beef, would they? So if you can say no on religious grounds, why can't you say no on grounds of health?

While it's not advisable to open yourself up to temptation too early on in the weight loss programme, there will be times when you are obligated to attend social functions. But if you're worried that saying an outright no will not work, no matter how polite you are, we've devised some tactics to confront these tricky situations so that the only person you eat to please is you.

PREPARE

If you're trying to be disciplined about your eating, you can forget about finding healthy food at parties. By and large, rich food is the focus of social events.

Tank up on soup and salad before going. You'll feel fuller and won't end up overeating, maybe you won't feel like eating at all. If you still feel hungry, you can stick to a few small portions (of the healthier options).

And if the diet doesn't come to you, bring the diet to your friends. carry your healthy dish to the party – enough for everyone, not just yourself. You can take salads and other low-cal dishes and put them on the table next to the creamy dips and fried food. That way you can still eat healthy for most of the evening and your host will appreciate the effort you have made. Everybody wins.

APPRECIATE

When someone wants you to eat food they made or to eat at an event they are hosting, what they really want is for you to appreciate the effort they have made. They want you to compliment aspects of the dinner or the event, be it the presentation, the ambience or the taste.

You could say things like, 'Wow, this must have taken so long. I am so touched you put in all this effort for us/ me,' or 'You have really outdone yourself this time, the place, table and food look fabulous!' or 'You are such a wonderful hostess! I am having a great time!'

Also, compliment the food early and often. The more you compliment the dishes, the more people will think that you have eaten a lot – even when you haven't. Eat slowly but compliment after every bite. 'Mmmm... this chicken is just delicious. I can't get over how good it tastes,' or 'The fish is unbelievable, I am in heaven,' or 'You have to give me the recipe for this macaroni bake. I am going to make it for my next dinner party!'

POSTPONE

This is an especially good tactic for dessert. Postpone eating rich desserts by saying that you are full now so you will eat it in a bit when you can really *enjoy* it. Chances are your host will not ask you the second time around, as he or she will be preoccupied with other guests. But if they insist, you can ask if you can take the dessert home with you. Whether you eat it at home or not is your little secret.

ASK

This is the simplest thing you can do. Ask. Tell your host beforehand that you are on a healthy eating programme, and that you might not be able to eat much at their house. And if it's a close friend, you can always ask them to cook something light for you. If they're a good friend of yours, they won't mind.

It's always better to enlist the support of your family or friends when you're trying to lose weight. Tell them you would appreciate their help. They will be much more obliging to leave you alone.

How to Say No at a Wedding

I don't know what it is about weddings but one thing's for sure – even if you're married to your diet, weddings can make you unfaithful to your healthy lifestyle. The variety of rich food and general opulence of the entire event make people feel it's their right to overeat.

But believe it or not, saying no at a wedding is one of the easiest things you can do. The hosts are usually too pre-occupied to even notice whether or not – let alone what – you have eaten! At the most, they will ask you if you have eaten. You can use all the tactics described above: you can postpone, appreciate and gush about everything from the flowers to the decor, and they will be happy that you attended.

But if you must eat, to avoid getting off your healthy meal plan, try to eat something wholesome before you go. At the event, try not to stand near the buffet: you might pick mindlessly at the food. Find a spot to chill and socialize, and make it an event to remember – for reasons other than what you ate. And do remember that at weddings, the food is not always that good but sometimes we eat for the same reason people climb Mount Everest – only because it's there.

WHEN FOOD IS THE FOCUS OF THE EVENT

When we are invited to weddings, dinners or parties, we feel that we have to eat because, in our head, food is the focus of the event. We have a tendency to ignore our hunger signals and eat when we are not hungry just because we strongly associate the event with food.

Food is not the focus of the experience: it's just one part of the experience. The other parts are the people, the conversation, the ambience, the entertainment. When you make food less important, you automatically end up eating less. It's really as simple as that.

One effective technique to enjoy social events without overeating or breaking your diet is to visualize yourself at the event – focus on the conversations, on having a good time with people. Visualize the event in detail – right from what you are going to wear and who will be present to how you will stick to your healthy meal plan, when you will get there, who you will speak to. Visualize what you will eat, the process of eating it and the feeling of enjoyment while eating it. Visualize yourself feeling great afterwards – feeling light and satisfied rather than bloated and guilty.

This kind of detailed visualization creates a memory imprint in your brain. It tricks your brain into thinking the event has already happened. So when you are at the actual event, your memory gets stimulated, you feel like you have been here before and you automatically tend to engage in the same behaviours as you did in your vision. Don't underestimate the power of this technique. What has worked for some of the world's most successful people will definitely work for you.

DEEPIKA PADUKONE'S CHECKLIST FOR EATING OUT

❑ Have you planned ahead? If you know you're eating out later and it could be a lavish affair, choose wisely earlier in the day to keep calories, fat, sugar and salt intakes under control.

❑ Can you eat at home? If you're going for a party where you know dinner is going to be served very late, eat at home before you leave.

❑ Can you learn how to say NO? Don't eat an extra course just to be polite.

❑ Can you be cool with wasting food? Don't eat just to finish some food that might get left over.

❑ Can you share? Think about sharing a course with a companion if the portions look large.

'I Have to Do the Food Justice'

You know the feeling. You reach the event or the restaurant and the doors open – either literally or figuratively – almost like the gates of heaven. Only, heaven here is lined with silver-domed dishes atop cute little burners. You feel like every dish is calling out your name – EAT ME, they all seem to say. Your heart beats faster, your sensory cues go into overdrive and you begin to feel the presence of God. What you're experiencing is buffet mania.

And it will pass.

Buffets are a classic example of 'eating with your eyes'. In other words, greed. The lure of perceived quality – so many attractive

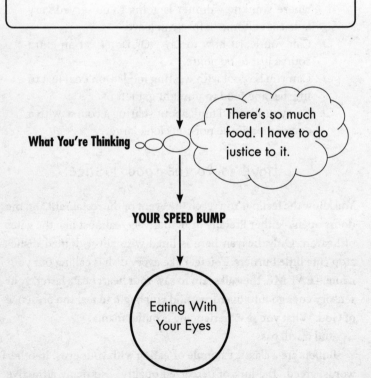

Situation

Buffet

What It Looks Like

ALL YOU CAN EAT @ 400 including a glass of beer.
TAXES INCLUSIVE!

What You're Thinking

There's so much food. I have to do justice to it.

YOUR SPEED BUMP

Eating With Your Eyes

dishes on display – coupled with the unbeatable temptation of unlimited quantities of food (all you can eat) can undo a week of weight loss in less than two hours. And yet, many don't even enjoy the food they are eating after the initial excitement – they are just finishing their food because they don't want it to go to waste.

The key to eating at a buffet is to make a distinction between what you want and what you *really, really, REALLY* want. Before you grab a plate – because this will hasten poor judgement – take a round of the table, like you are visiting an art show. Focus on the MF Hussains of the table – two or four masterpieces that you really must try – and leave the rest alone. You'd be surprised at what you bring back with you.

When you go shopping, you go with a broad idea of what you want to spend, right? If you see ten different dresses you like, you still need to make choices based on your budget. Just like clothes are not running away – you can always get them when you earn more money – food is also not running away.

It's also a question of need. When you focus on quality you don't need a whole lot to feel satisfied. In fact, after the first three bites, the law of diminishing returns sets in, and we don't enjoy the food as much as we did at the start! You don't need to eat everything in front of you. You can always try something different next time. You have to get out of thinking that you need to 'do the food justice'– it's food, and it's there to do *you* justice.

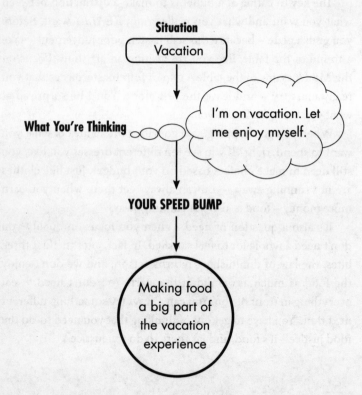

'I'm on Holiday'

Vacations are invariably tied to the feeling that you 'need' or 'deserve' them. And you do. Taking time off from the daily grind, recharging and reconnecting with your loved ones, beats the monotony of daily commutes, deadlines and everything else that spells stress. But holidays also make you think you need 'time off' from your healthy lifestyle. It's like you take a vacation from your diet because you equate that with your regular life and your trip becomes the all-or-nothing paradise where no rules apply.

It's not like you can't eat something unplanned when you're on vacation. But a no-holds-barred approach to food can make you feel tired and sluggish – not to mention heavier – leaving you to go back to your life with new problems and not the solution the break was meant to be.

The key to eating on vacation is not to make food the focus of the break. It's a new place, there are so many things to see and do, and if you stop thinking about food you can focus on so much more. You can walk, commune with nature, watch movies, play a sport, read, shop till you drop, sightsee, get spa treatments, or discover something new and different about the place or about yourself.

The point of a holiday is to relax, recuperate, unwind. It's not to overload and burden your digestive and other systems. Which is not to say that you can't eat your favourite foods, but the way you think about your holiday is important. If you go into your break thinking, *now I can eat what I want*, you will eat limitlessly and mindlessly whether you are hungry, thirsty or neither. Aim not to gain any weight – if you go with that intention, you'll be surprised at how easily you can stick to your plan.

Practise visualization techniques before you go. Visualize yourself getting into the plane, train or car. Feel the excitement as it starts to move, briefly signalling the end of your association with your old life. Picture the journey, arriving at your destination, being assailed by new experiences and new people. Focus on what you might see there – the shops, the landscape, the time you spend with your family or friends and the fact that you are completely switched off from life as you know it. Concentrate on the feeling of being relaxed, light and carefree.

Visualize yourself eating and not overdoing it. Picture yourself eating healthy and feeling satisfied. Imagining eating healthy and feeling good about it is important. Visualize as often as you can before your vacation, and you will already be mentally prepared to look at your break in a whole new light.

THE VACATION STRATEGY

Before You Leave

❑ Plan what you might be eating. Be determined to discover healthy eating options. Every cuisine has light and heavy eating options. Read up before you go or ask friends for recommendations or use the guide to eating out at the end of this book.

❑ If possible, make reservations at hotels or in places where there are gyms and restaurants which can make food according to your needs.

❑ Increase the time you spend doing physical exercise a week or two before you go. This will speed up your weight loss and increase calorie burn.

❑ Eat light a few days before you set off.

❑ Mentally prepare yourself not to gain weight.

❑ Carry a little food bag with you so that you can eat often. Dry portable snacks like biscuits, khakra, low-calorie snack bars, homemade roasted snacks, kurmura (puffed rice) and channa mix (in small zip lock bags, one for each day of travel) will keep you nourished on the go. Stock your hotel room/ holiday home with fresh local produce (carrot or cucumber sticks, low-cal crackers, small tetrapacks of yogurt. With these in hand you are equipped not only to combat hunger but also prevent binge eating.

When You're There

❏ Be a fussy eater. Ask for salad dressing on the side, or order pizza without cheese.

❏ Don't give in to social pressure to eat. Remind yourself that you are the only one eating for you. You want to feel good and not bad after overeating. Treat your holiday as a time for you to feel relaxed and not pressured into doing – or eating – something you don't want to.

❏ Eat only one heavy meal a day – it could be lunch, breakfast or dinner, your choice. Me? I'd eat a heavy breakfast because that way I'd be fuelled for the day and I would burn off most of it with all the walking around while sightseeing or shopping!

❏ You need your food diary more than ever when you're on vacation. Write down everything you eat as soon as you eat it. You will automatically start practising self-control.

❏ Walk everywhere and as much as possible. But don't think that just because you are walking more than you do at home, you can eat what you want. Most of us – even nutritionists – overestimate how much we burn and underestimate how much we eat. Your walking will only help counter what you are currently eating.

❏ Drink plenty of water – a crucial tip that is usually ignored on holidays. Studies have shown that UTIs (urinary tract

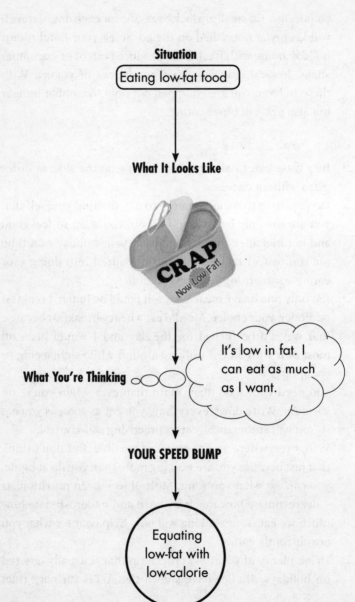

infections) are far more common in individuals during or after holidays, primarily due to lack of adequate water intake.

When we go on holiday, we don't let go of our budgets. We don't neglect our kids or stay unconcerned about how they occupy their time. We don't forget to brush our teeth or make reservations. We control ourselves in so many situations even while we're on holiday, so why is it okay to let go when it comes to food?

'It Says Low-fat on the Pack'

Even if you're good at math, it's a calculation that most don't get right. The mentality 'because-it's-low-fat-I-can-eat-as-much-as-I-want' can derail even the best weight loss efforts. And here's why:

❏ *Low-fat doesn't always mean low-cal*. It may be low in fat, but a lot of these foods are pumped with sugar to taste good. Read the nutritional label to get an idea of the calorie content, and see if it makes sense to eat it in the first place.

❏ *It still has calories*. Even if fat-free foods are low in cal, they still have calories. So if you eat 10 biscuits of 20 calories each, you may as well have had 4 × 50-calorie biscuits; the intake is the same. Bear in mind that water is the only zero-calorie food that exists.

❏ *Some low-fat, low-cal foods lead to cravings in the long run*. This is especially true for drinks that use sugar substitutes or artificial sweeteners, which enhance your appetite and ensure that you feel hungry later or crave sugary, unhealthy foods.

❏ *Fat-free or low-cal doesn't make it healthy*. Your body is meant to be nourished. Just because it's low-cal doesn't mean it's healthy. You don't want to eat only for the calorie value, you want to eat for quality value.

Situation

Dieting in Public

What You Think It Looks Like

Did you see Mallika? She was saying no to all the starters. Is she on a diet? Is she trying to get into that LBD for new year's eve? Fat chance!

What You're Thinking

Weight loss comes so easily to my friends. I don't want to look like I work on it.

YOUR SPEED BUMP

Eating to prove a point

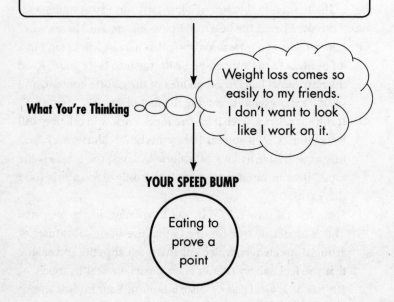

What this means is that you don't have to completely ignore all low-fat foods (as long as they meet your nutritional and calorific requirements, they are fine). It's just that you might need to tread with caution and think before you tear into the next packet that is cheekily labelled 'fat-free banana chips'.

'I Don't Want to Look Like I'm Dieting'

Of all the reasons for you to stray from your healthy diet, eating to prove a point has to be one of the most unnecessary. To deal with this situation, I would like to introduce you to two words that should stay with you through your weight loss and maintenance phases; two words that will give you the freedom to be answerable to no one. And those two words are...

WHO CARES?

Like eating to please, when we break our healthy diet because we are embarrassed about being on a diet, we often overestimate or assume what the other person is thinking. We feel so overwhelmed by a sense of shame that we eat because we want to prove to our friends that we don't need to make the effort to stay in shape. We also assume that other people are busy thinking about us. But we needn't worry. They aren't.

And who cares what anyone thinks? It's not that you can't make excuses. You can say you can't drink because you are taking antibiotics or that you are detoxing for a bit, but in the long run, you should feel comfortable with the idea of saying no. You don't have to make a big deal out of it; a simple shake of the head when the starters are being passed around should suffice.

If anyone probes – and they probably won't – just say you want to eat healthy for a bit. And if you really want to be one up, you can sell the idea of healthy eating to them. Brag about how much more energized you are feeling, how much better your clothes fit and how much more you can get done in a day. Chances are, you might convert a few people and set *them* on the right path.

Finally, don't assume that nobody works out or has their own way of keeping their weight down. Nearly all your friends will be doing something or the other to maintain their bodies. But even if they are not always as forthright as you are, they probably envy the confident, carefree and honest way you go about your new lifestyle.

SONAM KAPOOR'S CHECKLIST FOR EATING ABROAD

❏ Can you carry snacks in your bag? It doesn't matter where you are or in which hotel you stay, you can always carry fruit or nuts in your bag.

❏ Can you drink more water? Try and drink lots of water when you're on vacation or travelling abroad. You're walking around more and you need to stay hydrated.

❏ Did you know it's far easier to find healthy food than you think? When I'm abroad, I find that it's no problem to find healthy food. Unless you want to have Indian food, the best option is to have sandwiches or choose food that's grilled.

Eating Out

You Don't Have to Curb Your Lifestyle

While we have talked about not making food the centre of your life, you can't be expected to spend your life locked away in the safety of low-oil ghar ka khana. Hidden in restaurants are some healthy and nutritious diet gems, which provide you with a welcome change from time to time, although I wouldn't recommend this more than once a week if you're in the weight loss phase. To get an idea of proportions, please refer to your meal plan and eat as per the allotted quantity.

I've spent a large part of my professional life – and quite a bit of my vacation time! – investigating the healthiest and unhealthiest meal options world cuisines have to offer. For the sake of convenience, I recommend that you cut out this section, carry it around in your purse, wallet or pocket, so that you can always make the right choices at the right time.

Enjoy.

ITALIAN

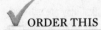

✓ ORDER THIS

- Minestrone soup
- Chicken Marsala
- Grilled salmon
- Chicken or fish – grilled, baked or broiled with lemon sauce on the side
- Rocket leaves or arugula salad – reduce or completely eliminate the goat cheese and order vinaigrette dressing (especially citrus vinaigrette like lime, lemon or orange) on the side
- Pasta – of any kind. It could be penne, spaghetti or linguini in tomato or marinara sauce. Ask the chef to reduce the olive oil and eliminate the cheese. Do try and ensure that your pasta dish has an equal proportion of pasta and vegetables. You can also add chicken, fish or turkey if you like.
- Clay oven pizzas work well with your new lifestyle. You can order the pizza with tomato sauce, fresh basil and your choice of vegetables, chicken, seafood, fish or turkey (please avoid bacon, ham, sausages and pepperoni) and ask the chef to make your pizza with no cheese or as little as possible!
- Cappuccino with skimmed milk
- Fruit sorbet – ask for no added flavours or syrups

NOT THIS

- Caesar salad – if you think this is real Italian food, think again. It's an American invention with rich creamy dressing, fried croutons and loads of parmesan.
- Fettuccine alfredo/ bolognese – alfredo is a heavy cream or white and cheese sauce while bolognese is a heavy meat-filled red sauce.
- Lasagna/ Ravioli/ Cannelloni – high fat preparations, which use cream and cheese as key ingredients.
- Eggplant or Chicken parmigiana Parmigiana is the same thing as parmesan so again, it'll be loaded with cheese.
- Fried fresh calamari – anything that's deep fried is a no-no.
- Gelato
- Tiramisu – it's rich in liqueur and uses mascarpone cheese as a chief ingredient

At any point if you don't understand what's inside the dish, just ask the server. They will be more than happy to translate for you.

CHINESE

The best thing about both Chinese and Japanese cuisines is that they are extremely healthy and probably the most suited to your weight loss programme. However, the chicken and veggies are usually deep-fried before the sauce is added. So make sure you ask the chef not to deep-fry. Choosing wisely just depends on the choice of sauce and the technique of cooking. Wherever you go, you can ask the chef to make your dish fit your needs. All you have to do is ask.

 ORDER THIS

- Chicken/ prawn/ vegetable suimai
- Seafood or vegetable cheung fun
- Prawn/ chicken/ vegetable dimsum
- Steamed bread or mushroom/ chicken bun
- Tum yum soup
- Wanton soup
- Chicken/ vegetable noodle soup
- Steamed rice – fried rice is, well, fried.
- Soft stewed rice with vegetables
- Soft stewed noodles
- Steamed prawns in lemon sauce
- Steamed fish in soya, ginger, spring onions
- Chicken/ prawn/ exotic vegetables in Hunan sauce or Oyster sauce – ask the chef to ensure that the vegetables, chicken or fish is boiled or sautéed and not deep-fried

NOT THIS

- Fried wantons
- Steamed dimsum in chilly oil
- Peking duck
- Pork bun
- Salt and pepper fried chilly prawns
- Fried chilly chicken
- Sesame prawn toast
- Szechwan chicken
- Chicken/ fish/ vegetarian Manchurian
- BBQ spare ribs/ Chinese spare ribs – spare ribs are basted in sauce that is high in both sugar and fat.
- Kung pao chicken/ potato
- Chow mein and lo mein
- Golden fried prawns – anything with the word 'golden' in it is fried
- 'Crispy' spinach chicken
- Black bean chicken
- Spring rolls
- Butter garlic prawns/ chicken/ vegetables
- Fried rice of any kind
- American chopsuey

Most Chinese restaurants also have sauces at the table. The classic soya sauce and chilly vinegar are healthy enough, but avoid anything with oil (and you'll know it when you see it) as it could completely set all your efforts back!

JAPANESE

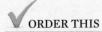 ORDER THIS

- Sushi – especially Nigiri Sushi (rice and seaweed) made with cooked crabs, salmon, bass, yellowtail, tuna, squid, scrambled eggs, tofu or vegetables
- Sashimi – raw salmon, tuna, squid or prawn
- Maki rolls – with no cheese
- Miso soup
- Oshinko – pickled vegetables
- Steamed edamame
- Teppanyaki dishes – ask that they are prepared with no oil. You can order these dishes with chicken, fish or vegetables.
- Sukiyaki dishes – these are cooked at the table and you can monitor the oil content.
- Okonomiyaki pizza – 'Okonomi' = anything you like and 'Yaki' = cook or fry, so use your power!
- Broiled sea bass (or any fresh catch of the day) with soya or ginger sauce
- Ocha or green tea – as much as you like!
- Soba noodles

NOT THIS

- Tempura – this is nothing but a Japanese pakoda. Anything that's 'tempura' is batter-coated and deep-fried.
- Dragon roll
- Chicken Teriyaki
- Yakitori
- Fried dumpling or Gyoza
- Ramen noodles
- Breaded chicken katsu
- Green asparagus tempura or sautéed with soya butter
- Foie gras teppanyaki
- Sake

LEBANESE, MEDITERRANEAN

 ORDER THIS

- Baba ghanoush – without the extra olive oil drizzle
- Hummus
- Tzatziki
- Greek salad – with reduced feta cheese. Ask for the dressing on the side.
- Horiatiki salad – this is nothing but tomato, cucumber and olives with vinaigrette dressing. Ask for less feta and dressing on the side.
- Souvlaki
- Dolmades
- Keftedes – essentially Greek meatballs, Keftedes work if they are baked and not fried.

NOT THIS

- Moussaka – because it contains high-cal beef and cheese
- Pastitsio – a heavy Greek casserole with pasta, beef, cheese and béchamel sauce
- Spanakopita – spinach pastries
- Deep fried calamari
- Tiropita – cheesy, and how!
- Falafel
- Red pepper feta
- Saganaki cheese
- Gyro platter – this includes beef and lamb and lots of grease!
- Baklava
- Baklava cheesecake

THAI

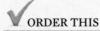 **ORDER THIS**

- Tom yum soup
- Po tak soup – clear seafood or vegetable soup with lemon grass
- Dom yang gung – hot and sour shrimp soup
- Chicken or fish satay – with the peanut sauce on the side
- Summer rolls
- Sam Tum – green papaya salad
- Cucumber salad – ask that the sweet and sour sauce be on the side
- Grilled chicken in Thai seasoning
- Gaeng pah – these water-based spicy curries serve as a low-cal substitute to the high-cal coconut based ones
- Pad thai noodles – ask for the noodles to be prepared in low oil and eliminate the peanuts entirely
- Pad see ew – broad flat Thai noodles, steamed with boiled chicken and/ or vegetables with soya sauce

NOT THIS

- Thai coconut soup
- Tom kha kai
- Spring rolls
- Curry puffs
- Crab Rangoon
- Money bags
- Pla mouk tad – fried calamari
- Pla lard prik
- Massaman curry
- Panang chicken
- Kao Pad – Thai fried rice
- Mee Krob – crisp fried noodles
- Spicy basil fried rice
- Sweet coconut rice

MEXICAN

 **ORDER THIS**

- Black bean or pinto bean (not refried beans) burritos – with loads of veggies, and a dash of guacamole. Don't go overboard on the guacamole. Avocados may contain 'healthy fats', but at the end of the day fats are fats, when you're trying to lose weight, it's better to avoid them in large quantities all 'fats' add calories. Enjoy this dish with salsa and not sour cream.
- Use salsa as a garnish, dressing, topping, dip or side to save loads of fat calories, as opposed to nacho cheese or sour cream.
- Chicken or vegetable fajitas – hold the cheese!
- Seviche – this is fresh fish or shrimp cooked in lime juice and is a really healthy, delicious option
- Quesadillas – ask that they are dry roasted with no beef and with reduced cheese
- Pico de gallo
- Gazpacho – this is a nutritious, tomato-based vegetable soup
- Enchiladas – if you're ordering enchiladas, get soft corn tortillas with chicken and vegetables, black bean and a little steamed rice! Avoid the cheese.

NOT THIS

- Nachos
- Flautas or Taquitos
These soft tortilla wraps are full of meat and are deep fried.
- Chalupas – these thick fried shells are filled with meat and cheese.
- Chimichangas – these deep fried burritos won't do your healthy lifestyle any good.
- Beef burritos
- Refried bean burritos
- Chorizo
- Taco salad
- Crunchy tacos
- Pitcher of margarita!

NORTH INDIAN

Indian cuisine is packed with flavour but loaded with vegetables, pulses, yogurt, rice and other cereals making it inherently healthy! However, the use of spice, which is the backbone of our cooking, enhances flavours making it compatible with low-oil preparations.

 ORDER THIS

- Tandoori roti or naan (no butter)
- Roomali roti
- Steamed rice
- Yellow dal – ask for no tadka; this request will be fulfilled at any Indian restaurant whether it's a small dhaba or a five-star hotel
- Tandoori or grilled mushroom/babycorn/ cauliflower/ paneer – request for no basting with butter on top
- Tandoori chicken/fish/prawn tikka – request for no basting after removal from the tandoor
- Green salad, kachumber, raita
- Roasted papad
- Green chutney or water-based pickle
- Masala chhaas

NOT THIS

- Plain/stuffed paratha, butter naan/roti
- Pulao, biryani
- Dal makhani, dal fry
- Samosa, pakora
- Butter chicken/paneer
- Malai kofta, methi mattar malai
- Palak paneer
- Raan
- Fried masala papad
- Oily aachar, sweet chutney
- Chicken or vegetable jalfrezi/ achari/
- Fish koliwada or any fried fish
- Cream based masala curry
- Boondi raita

 SOUTH INDIAN

ORDER THIS

- Idli, paniyaram, idiyappam
- Sambhar
- Rava idlis
- Sada dosa, rava dosa, neer dosa, lapsi dosa, ragi dosa (less oil/butter)
- Tomato uttapam
- Appam
- Curd rice, lemon rice, tamarind rice
- Rawa upma
- Cabbage poriyal
- Avial – no coconut oil
- Pongal – without ghee

NOT THIS

- Coconut chutney with vaghar
- Ghee idli, Kanchipuram idli, fried idli, Chettinad idli
- Medu wada, dahi wada, dal wada, sambhar wada, rasam wada
- Puri korma/ bhaji
- Mysore masala
- Masala dosa with cheese
- Sandwich uttappam with cheese
- Chettinad biryani
- Sheera

Ladies and gentlemen, welcome aboard. Your body weight is now in cruise control. Kindly unfasten your seat belt because it is too loose for you anyway. Should you hit rough weather, kindly refer to the maintenance manual so that you are always in the best shape of your life...

Your Autopilot

When planes first started appearing in the sky, pilots monitored every second of the journey. But as distances got greater and long-haul flights began to multiply, it became increasingly difficult for pilots to work for hours at a stretch. Autopilots were pressed into service – technologies to ensure that after a certain point, the plane safely flew itself.

Maintaining the weight you have lost is like putting your body on autopilot. Cruise control. All you have to do is put some checks in place, and you can get on with your life. But this is where many of us crash-land because we fly into an off-the-diet zone, resuming the same habits that made us gain weight.

But this is something we all know. In theory. So why is it that so many of us are unable to keep the weight off? Well, anyone can make you lose weight. But it's the 'off-the-diet' mentality which kills all those months of hard work and discipline – on again, off again, on again, off again. Have you ever wondered why you did that? Could it be that:

1. You thought once the weight was off, it needed no more help from you?
2. You didn't know how much you could eat?
3. You thought you could never eat the things you liked?

ONE   Your new body is like a new car; you have to get it serviced regularly if you want to keep it in optimum condition. You have to work to stay in shape because it's a new body you're maintaining. If you resume your old eating habits, you are maintaining your *old* body and not your new one. So what you did to maintain the excess 15 kilos, for example, will not work when your body is 15 kilos lighter – your needs are different. When you abandon healthy eating after you have lost weight, it messes with your system. For one thing, you start gaining the weight back. Two, and most importantly, with every kilo you regain, you lose the battle in your mind; you feel that after this much effort if you can't eat everything you want, what's the point? The point is that your weight is finally where it needs to be. You're feeling lighter, you're breathing easier, you're healthier, you have a lot more energy and your body is thanking you for it every single day. And you *can* eat everything you want – you just have to do it smartly and incorporate it into your lifestyle.

TWO   You'd be surprised at how much you can eat to maintain weight. In the active phase, you were eating less than your BMR. Now you can eat more *and* include the things you had cut off like dessert and cheese. And this is where I come in with a three-step guide that tells you how to get all you want back into your life.

THREE   You'd be surprised at *what* you can eat. I'm reproducing the list of foods from 'Break Up With Your Food Past' so that you get a broad idea of what you can re-integrate into your system. Which is basically everything.

Best Friends
What you can eat on a daily basis

Rice Roti Bread Upma Kurmura **Dalia**
Cornflakes **Popcorn** Noodles Poha Bhel
Spaghetti Wholewheat pasta Vegetables Potato
Peas Chicken Fish **Turkey** Dal **Moong** Channa
Rajma **Grapes** Mangoes Bananas **Paneer**
Skimmed milk Curd **Egg white** Quinoa
Khus khus Sweet Potato Rava Sooji Bajra Jowar
Rahi **Biscuit** Momo

Good Friends
You can hang out with these once or twice a week

Cheese Dessert **Chocolate** **Muffin** Fried food
Pizza Prawns Cake Ice-cream **Samosa**
Batata vada **Pakoda** Fried wanton **Jalebi**

Acquaintances
You can air-kiss these foods once a month

Lard **Bacon** Beef Mutton **Pork** Shellfish
Smoothie Fruit juice Aerated beverages
ANYTHING ELSE YOU WANT!*

Now that you've sowed the seeds in the active phase and increased your BMR, it's time to smartly enjoy the food you like, without worrying about it showing on your scale. So, ladies and gentlemen, without further ado, welcome to the Autopilot's Guide to Your New Body.

* This is just a rough list and is not exhaustive. The point of this is to give you a general idea of frequency of consumption.

NO SUGAR IN TEA AND COFFEE

There's no way I can put this sweetly. STOP ADDING SUGAR TO YOUR TEA AND COFFEE. It is a completely useless habit and one that leads you to thoughtlessly pile on the kilos.

But what's a teaspoon or two a day, you ask. Isn't that like having dessert? And don't I get dessert back in my life in the maintenance phase of the programme? Well, look at it this way – tea and coffee are always going to be a part of your life. If you have, on an average, two cups of tea a day (and most people have far more) and add a teaspoon of sugar to each cup, you consume 10 grams of sugar or 32 calories per day. That's 3.3 kilos gained in a year! Or at least, that's 3.3 kilos more that you have to work off in the gym!

Even if you consume the equivalent in artificial sweeteners, you are ingesting so many chemicals for the duration of your life! If you have two cups of tea a day, one or two pills/ sachets at a time, that's 1 pill/ sachet × 2 cups × 365 days × so many years ahead. Sweeteners extracted from the Stevia plant are the only exception.

And it's not just about the quantity of the calories, it's about the quality. Sugar adds empty calories. A gulab jamun may have sugar, but it also has carbohydrates and proteins, so at least there is *some* nutritive value. Sugar in your tea and coffee gives you *no* nutritive benefits at all.

If you think this is something you can never do, just give yourself a few weeks. Once your palate has adjusted to the new taste of your sugarless tea and coffee, you will never want to add sugar again.

The Autopilot Manual

ALWAYS HAVE ENOUGH FUEL

The principles of nutrition don't differ in the active and passive phases. Food is a vital nutrient and you need it as much in the weight loss phase as you do when you are finally maintaining your weight. The only difference between the active phase and the autopilot or passive phase is that in the former you were eating a little less than your BMR. In the latter, you're maintaining weight, so you don't need to cut any calories. Just eat according to your new body or, in other words, your new BMR.

FUEL YOURSELF

If you *never* want to go back to the dietician, you need to maintain the frequency of eating. As the aim is to ensure that your body is constantly burning, and your digestive system is in the 'gym', you need to keep eating every two to two-and-a-half hours for maximum impact.

DO A ROUND TRIP

Just because you've lost weight doesn't mean you need to give up your healthy exercise habits. In the passive phase, my clients walk or exercise four times a week to keep the weight off.

AVOID TURBULENCE

CELEBRATE! This is where the cakes, the cheeses, the nuts, the fried stuff can *all* be brought back into your life! You can eat *whatever* you want but there needs to be a balance. Your favourite foods need to be reintroduced to your system *slowly*. Reintroducing high-calorie foods systematically over a period of time will train your mind and body to get used to burning them off. Your body has to come to terms with your new weight; in other words, maintain your new weight *with* the high-calorie foods. Which is why my approach to maintenance is carried out in three stages.

Phase I: BMR + Dry Fruits or Nuts (20 grams of Nuts and Dry Fruits)

First | Calculate your new BMR.

Second | Take the sample diets as given for your new BMR. So, if your new BMR is 1350 calories, refer to the 1200 to 1400 calorie diets in the active section. Remember, you were cutting 100 calories earlier, but you don't need to do that any more as you are now simply maintaining what you have lost.

Third | Add approximately 20 grams of nuts and dry fruits (in total) to your meal plan every day.

When you have maintained your weight in this fashion (give or take 300 grams) for a minimum of one month, you can move on to the next phase.

Phase II: BMR + Dry Fruits or Nuts + Cheese or Fried Items

In Phase II, in addition to the above, add cheese OR fried items to your diet twice a week. That is, a slice of low fat cheese OR fried items (5 or 6 medium-sized pakodas/ 1 small batata vada/ 1 small medu vada) can be eaten twice a week. Alternatively, you could have one slice of low-fat cheese *and* your favourite fried food once each in the week. Additionally, you can add the yolk of one egg per week.

However, the important thing to note is that the fried food or cheese needs to be eaten as a snack and not with meals. That's the only way it can effectively be burned. You remember what we chatted about in the 'Trust' section? About how your body can burn only so much food at one time? If you eat fried stuff or cheese as a standalone snack, your body will be able to burn it far more quickly. Eating it with meals will lead to it being stored as fat.

When you have maintained your weight (again, give or take 300 grams) for 30 days, you can move on to the next phase of maintenance.

Phase III: BMR + Dry Fruits or Nuts + Cheese or Fried Items + Dessert

This is the last month of maintenance and this phase will mark how you maintain your new weight for life! You can add dessert to your diet now, including sugar-based desserts (jelly, custard, rice kheer, rasagulla, gajar ka halwa), twice a week. But this goes down to once a week if you have sugar and fat-based desserts(cheesecake, cake, ice-cream, gulab jamun). If you have sugar and fat-based desserts, you need to cut one fried food and one dessert from your diet per week. When you have maintained your weight for 30 days, your body is on autopilot and you have effectively set your eating patterns for life!

DON'T BE FUELLED BY TOO MUCH – OR TOO LITTLE – OIL

This is something that needs to be followed for the rest of your life. While the exact amount of oil should not exceed 1 to 4 teaspoons per day, it should never be less than that either. However, this is a general estimate, and could exceed or reduce based on your recent blood report or lipid profile. But don't worry, this oil allowance does not account for fried items and dessert. Further, if all your lipid parameters are normal, ghee and butter can be included in the per day oil quota.

DON'T FORGET TO CHECK IN

Weigh yourself once a week, on the same day, wearing similar clothing and at approximately the same time. It is the best way to monitor gains in weight and to ensure that you are on the right track.

If You Are Gaining Weight

DON'T PANIC!

Your weight can fluctuate up to 500 grams and sometimes even up to a kilo on a day. There are many reasons for these fluctuations: water retention, the onset of menstruation in women, constipation, eating late at night. For example, if you usually eat dinner at 8 p.m., but eat at 12:30 one night, you will weigh more the next day. These

fluctuations are nothing to be worried about. But if you are at the
same weight for more than a week, it can no longer be counted as
a fluctuation, and must be attributed to weight gain.

IN CASE OF TURBULENCE, FLY AT A LOWER ALTITUDE TILL THE COAST IS CLEAR

If, at any point, you gain weight during the maintenance phase,
go one step down. For example, if you're gaining weight in Phase
I, you need to go back to the last meal plan in the weight loss
phase before maintenance and lose the weight gained before you
return to Phase I. Similarly, you need to scale down from Phase
III to Phase II if you're gaining weight in Phase III. Remember
this golden rule: when you hit turbulence, all you have to do is go
down a notch. But don't worry about it, your weight will stabilize
eventually.

UN-SWEETEN YOUR HABITS

There is already a lot of sugar in your food plan: dessert, fruit,
chocolate, cake, ice-cream. So you can continue to lay off the
sugar in your tea and coffee in your maintenance phase. It won't
be difficult– your habit has been set!

FUEL YOURSELF DIFFERENTLY IN DIFFERENT TIME ZONES

Eat less as the day progresses. So if you have three rotis for lunch,
cut one down for dinner. This is primarily because your body is
winding down for the day, which means lower activity levels and
less calorie burn.

Promise Yourself

Weight loss isn't just about the weight. It's about you telling your body what to do, instead of your body telling you what to do. It's about freedom. If you want to climb that mountain, you can. If you want to run that marathon, you can. If you want to get into a fabulous pair of jeans, you can. Weight loss doesn't just give you the ability to look or feel your best. It gives you the ability to choose, call the shots and be the CEO of your life.

The end of this book also marks the beginning of a new, fantastic and fabulous journey to a healthier, sexier you. But before I let you go, I want you to make a few promises to yourself.

Promise yourself that you will set aside time to heal your body. That you – at certain times during the day and during the week – will put yourself ahead of your family, your friends, your work, your children.

Promise yourself that no matter how overwhelming life gets, you won't forget that your body needs to be fuelled. Every day.

Promise yourself that you will *never* make a choice between your health and your ideal body. That you will treat both with love, care, tolerance and patience. Especially love.

Promise yourself that no matter how many times you fail, you will forgive yourself. That no matter what people say, you will pick yourself up and resume your journey because you are answerable to nobody but YOU.

Promise yourself that you will always love yourself. That you will silence the voice in your head that doesn't think you are beautiful. And sexy. And wonderful. And special.

Promise yourself that no matter what you currently weigh, you will always believe that you are so much more than your body. That you will never allow your qualities, talent, nature and skills to be defined by the numbers on the scale.

Promise yourself that you will enjoy the journey. That you will relax, laugh and have fun during the process. That you will take your time to lose weight. That you will find new recipes, creative ways to exercise and make new friends with a shared interest in health. That you will discover the wonders of your beautiful body and welcome with open arms a whole new world that is waiting for you to explore it.

Forget your past, relish your future and inject your present with joy and enthusiasm. Because life's too short to be half lived.

Pooja Makhija

For You

SUSHMITA SEN

As an actor, as someone who works in the profession of beauty and glamour, there is something I feel you should know. *Everything* you see in films, magazines and on TV is airbrushed, touched up or *made* perfect. There is no such thing as perfection. There is none. It doesn't exist. We are as flawed as anyone else. I wanted to write this because I wanted to tell you that it is pointless wanting to be someone else. You can be inspired by someone, but you shouldn't aspire to *be* them. Everybody's lives, their bodies, their mental capabilities, their psychological abilities are taken. It's like a home that is taken. You don't want their home. It's not who you were meant to be. Every mole, every stretch mark, every line, every pigmentation mark on your skin is yours. It's unique to YOU. Be the best YOU can be. Let go of wanting to be someone else because *no one* can ever come close to being YOU. If you want to lose weight and keep it off, the first thing you've gotta do is love yourself. It is only then that your body will begin to heal.

Whether we are actors or bankers or housewives or architects, what we all have in common is that we live in very stressful times. Whether the stress is caused by waiting for a bus that doesn't show up or a train that is overcrowded or having to deal with people who are constantly angry with each other, we live in a world where everybody is stressed about something. Eating right, therefore, is no longer a luxury, it's a necessity. That's one of the most important things I learned from Pooja – eating is less about the way you look, it's more about the way you feel. You feel good when you feel alive inside. And soon, your body reflects that.

When I put on 9 kilos a few years ago, I faced enormous criticism. Initially, I used to wonder, 'Wow! How can people be so worried about *my* weight?' But the truth is, when you shock your body like that – too much weight gain, too much weight loss – it shocks your system. Pooja got me into this beautiful habit of eating right and eating every two hours, and at first my system fought back because I was still trying to get used to it. But soon you begin to understand the value of moderation. You begin to understand the value of balance. I never starve or try to suppress a craving or desire, but I don't overfeed it either. The body has a mind of its own. Listen to it. It will tell you what to do.

I dance to keep fit and I don't do this at a fitness club or with a personal trainer. I dance with my children. I dance with a sense of abandon – my arms go where they want, my legs go where they want and there is a real sense of freedom when I do that. Because I'm around people who love me. They don't judge me – no matter how much of a monkey I am making of myself. To be in an environment where people don't judge you is beautiful for your body. *That* helps you love yourself and in doing so there are more chances of you losing your weight and coming back to your beautiful self without worries.

Losing weight is a process; it's ongoing. Depending on your body type and metabolic rate, things will take their own course. Patience is a big virtue. Forget everything science and man have developed, you have to turn to nature. You cannot have a child nine days after conceiving it. It's unnatural; it cannot be done. Nature tells you that it will take nine months. And just as we can't change the tide of the ocean and we can't change the seasons at our own will, we can't change the nature of our individual bodies. That teaches you that there is no quick fix.

When you look back, this entire thing will be a quick enough fix. To make it quicker than this is unnatural, and anything that's unnatural makes you unhealthy and, therefore, shortens your life. And I would love to see people live their entire lives – healthy, happy, rearing to go – with NO'BODY' ☺ putting pressure on them. Because there is no party, event or person to go to that is as important as living in the skin you're in.

Love and God bless,
Sushmita Sen

Contributors

One of India's most prolific mental health professionals, DR ANJALI CHHABRIA has been a practicing consultant and psychiatrist for the last 20 years. She received her MBBS from the JJ Group of Hospitals in the year 1985, later going on to earn a Diploma in Psychotherapies, followed by an MD in 1990 from the Nair Charitable Hospital in Mumbai. She has also been visiting faculty for many educational institutes all over Mumbai.

Dr Chhabria has spent her life educating and counselling people on healthy emotional behaviour and has worked diligently towards generating awareness for psychological wellbeing. She has conducted workshops on a whole host of emotional and mental health issues and has featured in some of India's biggest publications.

Started by Dr Chabbria, MINDTEMPLE is a counselling centre which caters to psychiatric, emotional and behavioural concerns in individuals. The center combines contemporary psychiatric and psychotherapeutic methods with traditional Indian integrative mind philosophies to help individuals resolve their concerns holistically. Mindtemple treats eating disorders, depression, anxiety and panic disorders, mood disorders, ADHD, sexual disorders, learning difficulties, age-related disorders (like dementia, Alzheimers and menopause), stress and substance abuse to name just a few.

MANSI HASAN is a clinical psychologist, who has been working with Dr Chhabria for the past 9 years. She conducts psychological assessment for personality, emotional, intellectual, vocational and learning concerns.

She also specializes in CBT (cognitive behavioural therapy) for adults and play therapy for children. Mansi currently works with Singapore International School as their Senior Counsellor, training staff with coping with different psychological issues. She has also been a counsellor for television shows like *Entertainment Ke Liye Kuch Bhi Karega*, *Indian Idol* and *Sach Ka Samna*.

PRIYANKA DOSHI FERNANDES is a clinical psychologist who has been working with Dr Chhabria for the past 5 years. She primarily handles psychological assessment along with counselling at Mindtemple. She specializes in teaching behavioral techniques to adolescents and young adults and helping them with personal and emotional development. She is currently a part-time counsellor for 'Kamla Raheja Vidyanidhi Institute For Architecture' and has also been a counsellor for the television show, *Sach Ka Samna*.

TARA MAHADEVAN is a nutrition and health psychologist, specializing in weight management and eating behaviour by applying the principles of cognitive behaviour therapy. She believes that you first need to think straight if you want to permanently lose weight, and her unique approach provides clients with all the necessary psychological tools and strategies. She helps clients deal with a variety of issues from differentiating between physical and non-physical hunger, dealing with cravings and temptations, practicing mindful eating, building will power, and finally forming a long term holistic wellness plan.

Tara has a Master's degree in Psychology from SNDT University, Mumbai and a Bachelor's in Psychology from Vassar College, USA. She is also an internationally certified Wellness Coach and Weight counsellor from Wellcoaches Corporation, USA, a certified Clinical Pediatric Obesity counsellor from University of San Francisco, USA, a certified Nutrition and Eating Behaviours facilitator from the Am I Hungry® Mindful Eating program, USA, a certified Fitness instructor from Reebok and ACSM (USA) and a certified Nutrition Specialist from BFY, Mumbai.

Acknowledgements

No book is an island. *Eat. Delete.* could not have been possible without the contribution of some truly inspirational people who were such amazing sources of support. A big fat thanks

to my husband **Ravi,** my pillar and strength, and my two angels **Ahaana** and **Amaira** – you are my world and you have made me the person I am today.

to my wonderful **mom** and **ma**, thank you so much for being there when I couldn't. Thank you for putting up with me, my moods, my absence and my erratic schedules. Love and thanks also to my **dad, pa** and **Aakash** for being there when I needed you.

to my l'il sis **Ekta**, who has been my rock during this process. Thanks for all your notes, comments and for hitting me with a danda on the days when work overtook my book. And thank you for being my mirror and showing me what I was capable of. I could have never done this without you.

to my **clients**, who have made me the nutritionist I am today, thank you. You all inspire me to be the best I can be. Please keep smiling (and please keep eating every two hours).

to **Karthika** at HarperCollins for being such a receptive, fun and enthusiastic editor. It has been wonderful working with you.

to **Neelini Sarkar** at HarperCollins, for all your hard work in making this book what it is. Thank you for your eye for detail and for the true passion and commitment with which you work.

to **Tara Mahadevan**, nutrition and health psychologist, for your enthusiasm and support.

to **Dr Anjali Chhabria** for your invaluable inputs. I have learned a lot from you, doc! You rock!

to **Team Nourish** – as always you are indispensable, and I owe you a debt of gratitude.

And lastly, to my writer **Gayatri Pahlajani** for your passion, commitment and perseverance. Thank you for making this book your baby as much as it has been mine.

to the many people that I didn't include on this page, please do not think that I am not grateful. Thank you so much for being there and for being who you are.

Pooja Makhija